The
READINESS

Method

*Seeing Your Patterns,
Choosing Your Path*

*By
Karl-Heinz Schradt*

Email: galahbooks@hotmail.com or karls774@gmail.com
Website: thereadinessmethod.wordpress.com
YouTube: @READINESSwithKarl
TikTok: @readinesswithkarl

Published by: Readiness Press, Western Australia, Australia
ISBN: 978-1-7642424-9-3
Electronic format (Version 1): Jan 2026
Hardcopy: Feb 2026

Disclaimer:
The READINESS method, and all information associated with it — including content on websites, social media, videos, and other media — is intended for individuals who are emotionally stable, grounded, and able to bring clear awareness to their experiences. It is not appropriate for anyone currently experiencing conditions that compromise safety, judgment, or the ability to remain present and aware, including but not limited to severe emotional instability, acute distress, psychotic or dissociative episodes, active crises, or any situation that makes it difficult to stay in touch with reality.

This information and practice are not a substitute for therapy, professional advice, or medical care, and should be used only at your own discretion and risk. If you have any doubts, or if your situation involves safety concerns, please seek professional guidance before engaging.

Who is the Author?

Karl-Heinz (Karl) Schradt is a mental health professional and educator. He creates resources to help people navigate life's challenges and make their inner lives less complicated, more manageable, and more present.

In the future, he may offer workshops, talks, and one-on-one sessions, depending on demand and logistics. If you represent a community, service, or organization interested in having him speak, please feel free to contact him.

Table of Contents

Step One/ Overview

Step Two

Step Three

5

Book Overview
&
Step 1: Understanding
the Garden Analogy

Introduction to the READINESS Method

Q: What is The READINESS Method?

*A: "Readiness is a away of understanding the mind
that makes your inner life easier to deal with."*

Mental distress often begins before you know what it is.

A tightening in the body. A subtle unease in the mind. A low-level distress or quiet despair that appears without a clear cause. Shortly after, a story follows — an explanation, a justification, a familiar narrative that tells you what must be wrong or what must be done.

READINESS begins before that story.

Instead of fixing, judging, or obeying the impulse to act, you pause. You feel the breath. You notice the tension directly. Nothing needs to be pushed away. Nothing needs to be believed. As the body settles, a sense of safety returns — grounded, calm, and present.

From this calm, something important becomes possible: observation without interference. Over time, you begin to see patterns clearly — not as problems to solve, but as movements to understand. This is the foundation of the READINESS Method: simple presence that makes genuine choice possible.

Why This Matters

Doing what we have always done feels safe. Our nervous systems run countless automatic processes each day, and our capacity for conscious control is limited. Faced with uncertainty, complexity, and demand, staying on a familiar path feels coherent — even sane.

But sometimes the familiar path is no longer the right one.

Imagine an aircraft flying smoothly on autopilot. Everything appears stable, yet the destination entered into the system is wrong. The plane can fly perfectly — and still arrive somewhere unintended. Tension keeps us obeying old coordinates. Calm and presence allow us to check them.

READINESS does not force change. It creates the conditions in which change becomes possible, within your actual bandwidth.

Who This Is For

Have you reached a point where you know something has to change?

This may show up in work, emotional life, health, spirituality, philosophy, or the search for meaning. You may sense that something is holding you in place — an assumption about how life works, or an automatic habit that quietly prevents you from choosing differently.

The READINESS Method is a tool for recognising the signs of standing still: of living according to inherited rules rather than consciously chosen values. It works by treating distress, tension, and stuckness not as failures, but as signals — indicators of unseen rules that no longer serve you.

READINESS can be used to reduce ongoing distress, or to support stepping out of fear into new directions. It is not designed for those who are comfortable remaining in familiar routines. This is a personal decision point, and one that cannot be made on your behalf.

Please read the disclaimer carefully. This method is not suitable for individuals currently experiencing serious mental illness.

What This Method Is — And Is Not

READINESS is not a belief system. It is not a prescription for how to live. It does not promise happiness, success, certainty, or enlightenment.

It is written for those who sense that what once drove them no longer fits, and who want a way to relate more wisely to their experience without replacing one authority with another.

Everything about us — our habits, perceptions, values, and identities — is conditioned. Over time, some of what we learned becomes misaligned with who we are and how life actually unfolds. READINESS offers a way to examine this conditioning gently: to notice which patterns support you, which drain you, and how to soften what is no longer beneficial without destabilising your life.

The emphasis is not on drastic change, but on discernment. Not on becoming someone new, but on seeing more clearly how you are already being shaped — and reclaiming authorship where it matters.

A Final Note

You will not find claims here about ultimate reality, the nature of God, or how the brain really works. I will not tell you what to believe or who to become. I may invite you to investigate your own experience — and to trust what you find there. You remain in the driver's seat.

The READINESS Method is offered as a practical way to reduce unnecessary strain, protect your energy, and live with greater clarity and ownership — without turning your life upside down. This is not a path for everyone. But if something in you recognises this moment, then this may be the right place to begin.

Teaching Structure: Three Major Steps

I present the READINESS Method in three main steps.

First, I explain the process using a simple analogy. You are a gardener tending a garden that no longer serves you. In practical terms, this means recognising a mind that generates unnecessary anxiety and distress, and learning how to soften and turn down the patterns that create these difficulties.

Second, I describe a gardening process that is effective but gradual. In lived terms, this involves learning how to notice problems clearly and work with them skillfully, so they become less anxiety-inducing over time rather than something that must be fought or eliminated.

Third, I introduce the idea of the skillful gardener. Life is inherently challenging, and these challenges often increase as we age. The skillful gardener not only tends the garden and gently changes its direction over time, but also grows in understanding, discernment, and wisdom through the process itself.

I structure my teaching by first giving you an overview of the processes and frameworks—like this one. I then explain them briefly here in the book's introduction, so you can understand how the pieces fit together. Later in the book, each topic is explored in depth, with clear instructions and deeper discussion.

What follows is an outline of the teaching structure that forms the backbone of the entire book.

1. The Analogy

We begin with an accessible analogy. Your journey of inner restructuring is likened to working with a garden.

You inherit this garden from your recent past. It reflects previous conditions, habits, and decisions. Now, you are in a position to make it your own.

2. The Gardening Process — READINESS

Building on this analogy, we introduce the process of "re-gardening yourself" through a simple and memorable acronym: READINESS. The aim is for this process to be recallable anywhere, at any time, without reliance on tools, techniques, or external resources.

The acronym describes the basic actions involved in reshaping your inner garden with insight:

- Recognise problem plants, not only by how they appear, but by the difficulties they create in your life.

- Understand them: their origins, the conditions that sustain them, and why they no longer fit the kind of garden you are cultivating.

- Stop feeding them with attention, belief, or energy—or learn to trim them carefully so they gradually lose their strength.

This process is repeated with increasing clarity and depth. Over time, what once seemed necessary and solid begins to appear optional— something that no longer has real power or "teeth."

Remember, this is a metaphorical garden. The plants represent habits, thoughts, emotional patterns, and assumptions—not actual flora.

3. The Skillful Gardener

Finally, we turn to the skillful gardener. After observing and assessing the garden, you become someone who consciously fills the spaces left behind when old ideas and learned core beliefs are released. Understanding the task and learning the process are essential, but neither is sufficient on their own. The effectiveness of the method depends on the quality of attention and discernment brought to it.

Life is inherently challenging, and these challenges often increase as we age. The skillful gardener not only tends the garden and gently changes its direction over time, but also grows in understanding, discernment, and wisdom through the process itself.

Cultivating a skillful gardener involves:

- Developing a clear sense of direction and intention — knowing where your life is headed and what matters most.
- Establishing basic, reliable skills that become habitual — the foundations learned in Step 2 now support more fluid, responsive engagement with life.
- Gradually gaining deeper, experiential understanding through practice over time — insight begins to shape choices naturally, without conscious effort.

The skillful gardener expresses this stewardship through three complementary modes of cultivation:

1. Daily Tending — ongoing attention to the inner garden using the READINESS process. Subtle adjustments prevent old patterns from quietly reasserting themselves.
2. Periodic Alignment — stepping back to review and gently adjust the broader structure of your life so it reflects emerging clarity, values, and priorities.
3. Deep Cultivation — a slower, intentional engagement with meaning, values, relationships, and uncertainty. This is not a strategy or mandate, but the natural expression of insight embodied over time.

The goal is not perfection or control, but steady, attentive care. With this approach, the mind becomes less burdened by unnecessary distress and more capable of clarity, flexibility, and ease. Over time, insight, discernment, and these cultivation practices combine to support greater coherence, meaning, and freedom — not as ideals to achieve, but as qualities that emerge from living in closer relationship with reality.

We now expand on each of these three domains in detail. You can also see the process diagram at the end of Step One, which provides a simplified view of the whole progression from procedural regulation to experienced stewardship.

Step 1: Understanding the Garden Analogy

The Garden as Your Mind, Body, and Life

Think of your mind, body, and senses as a garden. Some days it may feel orderly, like a traditional English garden: tidy, well-kept, but somewhat lifeless. Other times, it feels chaotic, overgrown, or trapped under its own complexity.

Your garden reflects your past: the habits, beliefs, and routines you've inherited or absorbed over time. Some of these elements are beneficial, like shade trees or nourishing vegetables. Others—like poison ivy or thorny vines—quietly drain your energy or block growth. There may even be large, old trees—fundamental principles or long-held beliefs—that provide stability but also cast long shadows over areas you would like to cultivate.

The first step in creating a garden that serves you is seeing that you are the gardener. You begin to notice which plants bring life and which do not. The goal is not to bulldoze what exists, but to prune skillfully: keep what nourishes you, trim what no longer serves, and create space for new growth.

The Automatic Garden

Before the gardener arrives, the garden grows on its own. This is the automatic garden—habits, assumptions, fears, and inherited beliefs that shape your life without conscious attention.

It is not morally "bad"; it is simply unattended. When left unchecked, it can become labyrinth-like:

- Overgrown paths where you can't see clearly

- Thorny patches that trap you when you brush against them

- Hidden wells that quietly drain your energy

The automatic garden reflects the part of life that runs on autopilot. Its rules feel unquestionable, its obligations non-optional, and its patterns invisible—yet they quietly guide your choices, energy, and emotional state.

Why the Garden Becomes Automatic

When we do not observe, calm, or understand the roots of our inner life, certain patterns take control. Like an iceberg, the visible tip is what we notice consciously, while beneath the surface lie assumptions, habits, and inherited beliefs. These hidden structures shape how we react, decide, and live. What we experience directly is distress or discomfort in the moment; beneath that lie the seeds from which it springs.

Patterns tend to form around what we call core beliefs and truth claims. These are lessons you were taught either directly or passively—through relationships, media, education, culture, and other influences over time. They are propositions that are assumed or claimed to be absolutely true and imperative. While they may have practical utility or good reasons for being believed, they also have real limitations. These ideas are introduced here only as orientation; we will return to them later with greater nuance and practical guidance.

In READINESS, we change our relationship to these seeds. I will give examples, but it's important to be clear: we are not rejecting these beliefs, nor are we agreeing with them. We are manually adjusting our subscription to them. We can do this because no one can ultimately decide the validity of a truth claim or core belief except the person themselves.

Examples of truth claims include:

- "God exists and has rules for people."
- "Science is the best method for knowing, and untested things have less value."

Examples of core beliefs include:

- "Pleasure gives life meaning."
- "Only successful people have value."

The automatic garden is especially powerful because it feels safe. Following inherited rules or societal expectations offers stability, familiarity, and social reinforcement. But safety does not equal suitability. Life may appear "on track" outwardly, yet inwardly you may feel depleted, restless, or misaligned.

Energy Traps and Their Consequences

When we live according to unquestioned rules or beliefs, our lives can fill with energy traps—things we feel compelled to pursue in order to feel safe, successful, or acceptable. These can include:

- Achievements we feel obligated to reach
- Material acquisitions such as homes, cars, or status symbols
- Careers, promotions, or titles
- The belief that we must have a family, a business, or social recognition

None of these are inherently bad. The problem arises when they are pursued out of fear, conditioning, or inherited expectations rather than clarity about what truly matters.

Energy traps can also take subtler forms: the problem we endlessly overthink, the regret that causes insomnia, or the moment we replay again and again. In this way, anxiety, low mood, and panic are often deeply connected to inherited beliefs.

Left unattended, these patterns can lead to:

- Exhaustion from endless striving
- A sense of unfulfillment despite apparent success
- A neglected inner life and loss of curiosity
- Confusion about where your energy is going
- Living in survival mode rather than with meaning

Decades of following energy traps can dim the natural spark of curiosity, openness, and joy that many of us had as children. With discernment and conscious care, however, that spark can be protected, sustained, and even rekindled.

Why READINESS Matters

For many, following the pre-programmed map of life feels comforting. It is familiar, socially reinforced, and requires little questioning. Yet some of us sense that this is not enough. We feel called to examine whether the path we're on truly serves us.

The READINESS Method is designed for those who want a more authentic life. It helps to:

- Bring hidden processes into view
- Reduce self-deception
- Recognize energy-draining patterns
- Reignite and protect the inner spark

Change does not have to be dramatic. It begins with observation, reflection, and small, intentional adjustments. Over time, these accumulate, creating a garden that truly reflects your values, goals, and authentic self.

A Story of the Garden in Action

Consider Jim.

Jim grew up in a family where appearances mattered above all—wealth, titles, and respectability defined success. He internalized these messages and, for years, followed a path that did not fit his authentic self. Corporate life drained him. Stress, illness, and a sense of disconnection accumulated.

Eventually, Jim chose to change. He moved to a quiet farm, simplified his lifestyle, and pursued work that felt tangible and meaningful. He pruned the parts of his garden that no longer served him and nurtured what brought joy and fulfillment. Slowly, he reclaimed his energy, curiosity, and inner spark.

Chapter Summary

- The garden metaphor illustrates your mind, body, and life, showing how some habits and beliefs nurture growth while others drain energy.

- The automatic garden grows unattended, often without awareness, shaping decisions and energy.

- Energy traps arise from inherited or conditioned rules, leading to exhaustion and unfulfillment.

- The READINESS Method offers a framework to observe, understand, and begin pruning your garden thoughtfully, reclaiming energy and agency.

Step 1.1 Becoming the Gardener:
From Automatic Living to Conscious Care

In the previous chapter, we explored the automatic garden—habits, beliefs, and patterns that grow without attention, often draining our energy or blocking growth. Now we turn to the gardener: the conscious part of ourselves capable of observing, choosing, and shaping the garden.

Most of us move through life on autopilot, relying on ingrained routines and learned patterns. For many, this works well. But there are moments when automatic living no longer serves us—stress accumulates, life feels misaligned, or old habits prevent us from reaching meaningful goals.

It is in these moments that manual control becomes possible, through what psychology calls metacognition—thinking about your own thinking. The gardener is the part of you that notices patterns, pauses, and intentionally adjusts what is not working.

Safety and Stability Come First

Change does not mean uprooting everything at once. The garden has grown for years; some elements are deeply rooted and essential. Stability must come first, or interventions risk destabilizing your inner life—like flying a plane into the ground.

Instead, the gardener makes small, precise adjustments:

- Keep what supports and nourishes growth
- Trim or redirect what is overgrown or obstructive
- Observe how these changes affect the garden over time

For example, Jeff has an oak tree in his garden. It provides shade, stability, and support, so he does not remove it. But some branches cast too much shade where he wants flowers to grow. By pruning selectively, he allows light to reach areas where new growth is desired.

A lived example: Jeff's father instilled a strong value for an ordered and structured approach to life. This gives Jeff stability and helps him manage work and daily responsibilities effectively. However, when he tries to impose that same order and structure on his relationships, tension arises. By selectively "pruning" his attachment to order in certain areas—

while maintaining it in his work and financial life—he creates space for healthier, more flexible interaction with others.

This careful, measured approach is at the heart of the READINESS Method. It allows you to reclaim agency without sacrificing stability.

The Automatic Self vs. the Gardener

Understanding the distinction between the automatic self and the gardener is key.

- Automatic self: Operates unconsciously, reacting based on learned patterns, habits, and beliefs. It is efficient and often protective, but it can perpetuate outdated or unhelpful behaviors.

- Gardener: The conscious agent capable of observing, intervening, and making changes where necessary. This is your executive function—the part of you that can step back, notice a pattern, and choose a different response.

Some people are content letting the automatic self guide them. Others, sensing misalignment or fatigue, wish to cultivate more agency. For them, the gardener provides a practical, actionable way to author their life, step by step.

Notice how Jeff's pruning illustrates this distinction: he does not remove order entirely (automatic self) but brings conscious awareness to how and where it functions (gardener), selectively adjusting to promote growth in relationships.

The Role of Observation

Observation is the gardener's first tool. Before pruning, before intervention, we must see clearly what exists.

- Which habits drain your energy?
- Which beliefs limit your choices?
- Which routines nourish your growth?

Observation does not require judgment. It is simply noticing: "This part of the garden is overgrown; this part needs water; this area is thriving."

Through consistent observation, we develop metacognitive awareness—a practical skill that allows us to make intentional choices about what to maintain, adjust, or remove. READINESS is the process that enables non-judgmental observation, helping us see the whole iceberg without reacting impulsively.

Jeff's story demonstrates this in action: he notices the tension between structure and flexibility in his relationships and adjusts consciously, rather than acting purely out of habit or reaction. This is the essence of becoming a gardener—bringing awareness to what is, and choosing how to respond.

Incremental, Intentional Change

The gardener does not act out of fear or urgency. Change is incremental, guided by insight rather than reaction. Over time, these small interventions accumulate:

- Obstructive habits weaken
- Energy drains are reduced
- Awareness and clarity expand

The READINESS Method provides a structured framework for this process. It is not a formula for perfection, nor a promise of happiness or certainty. It is a practical guide for tending your inner garden, helping you navigate life with more clarity, presence, and agency.

Preparing for Action

Becoming the skillful gardener requires patience, practice, and honesty. You will:

- Notice patterns in your thoughts, emotions, and behaviors
- Observe which "plants" in your garden support growth and which do not
- Make small, deliberate adjustments
- Continue observing and refining over time

This is a process, not a one-time fix. Just as a gardener tends the same garden season after season, you will return again and again to your inner landscape, gradually building a garden that reflects your authentic self.

Chapter Summary

1. The gardener represents conscious agency and metacognitive awareness.
2. The automatic self operates on autopilot, efficient but not always aligned with what truly matters.
3. Observation is the first tool: noticing patterns, energy drains, and areas of growth.
4. Change is incremental and intentional, prioritizing stability while gradually reclaiming agency.
5. The READINESS Method provides a structured way to intervene in your garden without destabilizing it.

Step 2: An Overview of R.E.A.D.I.N.E.S.S

Note: This section explains why each part of READINESS exists, so you understand the overall aim. Do not apply these skills until you have read the later "How" sections, and apply them in the order presented.

The READINESS Acronym

We'll explore the READINESS method using a gardening analogy.

Step 2: R - Recognise with Calm (Overview)

Recognising means noticing what is not serving you. In a garden, this might be weeds or unwanted plants. In the mind, it appears as habitual reactions such as anxiety, hypervigilance, uncertainty, or persistent judgment of yourself or others.

To recognise is simply to notice and name what is not beneficial, or what needs to be observed and understood. In gardening terms, it's noticing a plant you don't actually want.

For instance, one might notice tension arising in social interactions without needing to act on it. Seeing a reaction clearly, without immediately responding, is the essence of recognition.

The Skill of Self-Observation

Self-observation (often called mindfulness) is the capacity to notice the unfolding of experience — in body, mind, and senses — as it arises. In READINESS, this capacity underpins the ability to recognise reactions without being swept away by them. It is a passive, non-active step: simply noticing what is present, without judgment or interference.

Recognise with Calm

Recognise works best when approached with calm. Calm allows us to notice reactions clearly without being swept away by them. In READINESS, calm provides the foundation for self-observation and effective recognition.

Step 2: E - Endure & Accept (Overview)

Note: This overview explains why each part exists so you understand the overall goal. Do not start applying these skills without reading the later 'How' sections, and follow them in order.

After Recognise, the next step in READINESS is Endure and Accept. This principle is about sitting with what arises in the mind, body, or senses without reacting, suppressing, or forcing it. Endurance creates the calm space needed to understand patterns and respond wisely. Other parts of READINESS are approached only after this foundation is in place.

Why Observation Matters

Experiences often point to deeper patterns or underlying beliefs. The same physical or emotional tension can have very different sources:

Example: You're sitting in a discussion with friends you trust. There's nothing to fix, prove, or do, yet you feel a tightening in your chest as they express opinions about religion or politics. You notice an urge to speak. The urge feels hot and tight, and it could stem from different sources:

- One possibility: a pattern related to "I must protect my group" — you may decide this is a reaction that isn't serving you and choose to restrain it.

- Another possibility: a hidden or subtle pattern related to "It's not safe to express my opinions" — something within you that may be explored or expressed over time.

At first, the important step is simply to allow the tension to exist without judgment or reaction. This calm, non-interfering space gives you the opportunity to notice the root of the feeling and decide for yourself whether it is something:

1. Non-beneficial — a reaction you choose to restrain or stop, or

2. Subtle / integrable — a pattern you choose to explore or express over time.

Acting or suppressing prematurely would obscure these distinctions. Enduring the experience allows clarity to emerge naturally.

The Principle Of Endure & Accept

Enduring reactive patterns without reacting or forcing them is central to READINESS. Like noticing an unwanted plant without ripping it out, sitting with discomfort calmly lets patterns soften, fade, or reveal their deeper significance over time.

Summary

Endurance lays the foundation for the rest of READINESS:

- We endure because we do not yet fully understand the experience.
- Calm, non-judgmental observation creates the space to notice and decide which patterns are integrable and which may be restrained.
- Only after this can other skills, investigation, and action be applied.

Step 2: D - Discern Danger (Overview)

Note: This overview explains why each part exists so you understand the overall goal. Do not start applying these skills without reading the later 'How' sections, and follow them in order.

For someone new to READINESS, don't worry about applying "Discern Danger" yet. At this stage, you are focusing on observing and understanding experiences through the process. Once you've practiced and tagged experiences, "Discern Danger" will become a practical tool to help you respond quickly and wisely.

"Discern Danger" appears in the READINESS acronym primarily for experienced practitioners. Its role is to help identify experiences that have already been "tagged" through the full READINESS process. Until something is fully tagged, we skip "Discern Danger," because we first need to work through the process to understand it.

Example tags might include:

- Beneficial = Follow / Act on
- Neither Beneficial nor Non-beneficial = No mental energy / reaction / action
- Non-beneficial = Do not react / follow

How It Works

Once experiences are tagged, we know how to respond to them. When a reaction arises, if we recognize and have tagged it, we can simply follow, ignore, or otherwise respond appropriately until change has occurred.

Why It Matters

Think of the mind as a garden. To cultivate it wisely, we need to discern which "plants" (habits, reactions, patterns) to nurture and which to stop feeding. This requires:

- Observing which experiences and reactions are beneficial and which are harmful.

- Contemplating and investigating these experiences to determine their true nature.

- Tagging genuinely non-beneficial experiences as "danger," so we can recognize and manage them appropriately through the READINESS process.

- Cultivating what is genuinely beneficial, based on observation and reflection, without unintentionally altering healthy patterns too quickly, which could create instability.

Over time, this discernment helps develop wisdom and clarity. As our understanding grows, we can make deliberate choices about what to cultivate, what to remain neutral toward, and what to avoid. By tagging harmful patterns as "Danger," we can reduce their energy and create a healthier mental "garden."

Defining 'Non-Beneficial' and 'Danger'

In Step 3, the Skillful Gardener, we examine in detail what it means for something to be beneficial or not. The definition is subtle and not always obvious. As we move through the process of READINESS, we often discover that what we previously believed was beneficial was not, and what we assumed was not — is.

For example, you may have been taught to "follow the rules," which keeps you safe but may also limit openness to new experiences. In that case, what appears beneficial can also become a problem.

At the beginning, we use a simple working definition of what is beneficial: actions that do not damage your or others' health, livelihood, mental well-being, relationships, and do not put you in legal or social trouble.

With this definition, drinking to excess would be non-beneficial, while being kind would be beneficial.

However, as we progress, we see that breaking old norms may be vital for your well-being. Ending a relationship, leaving a well-paying job, or stepping away from a religious community may initially seem unbeneficial, yet may be absolutely necessary for your path. Over time, the definition of what is beneficial becomes more personal, contextual, and dynamic — changing as you gain new information and insight.

Step 2: I – Investigate (overview)

Note: This overview explains why each part exists so you understand the overall goal. Do not start applying these skills without reading the later 'How' sections, and follow them in order.

Investigation is the next essential skill in READINESS. It is practiced only once you can Recognize, Endure, and Accept reactions without acting on or suppressing them. Calmness is central: it allows you to observe experiences with curiosity rather than labeling them simply good or bad.

Investigation has two conceptual stages:

1. Procedural Observation ("Be a Detective")
This involves noticing patterns of reaction:
   • Triggers – What sparks the reaction?
   • Maintaining factors – What habits or behaviors sustain it?
   • Underlying beliefs – What core assumptions drive it?

Example: Tension in the neck, fear of starting a task, or judgmental thoughts may all stem from a familiar belief, such as "I must have control," which underlies discomfort.

2. Contemplation
After observing patterns, consider their function: Do they serve your well-being, or the well-being of others? (The well-being of others is of equal importance.) Contemplation uses Socratic questioning—curious, systematic inquiry—to explore beliefs, uncover assumptions, and clarify which are genuinely beneficial versus learned or unnecessary.

Key Points to Remember

   • Investigation is finite, not ongoing rumination. Set aside time to observe, discern, and gain clarity, then return to living fully.
   • Its purpose is to help you decide how to relate to patterns in the future, not to endlessly analyze yourself.
   • Calm, systematic observation allows insights to emerge naturally, preparing the way for intentional reflection or release.
   • Our contemplation or analysis should never exceed our calm. If you are restless or overthinking, return to cultivating calm before proceeding.

Step 2: N-E-S-S of READINESS (Overview)

Note: This section explains the "why" of each part so you understand the overall goal. Do not start applying these skills yet — the practical instructions come later.

Over time, pre-programmed notions reveal their lack of substance. Drives rooted in conditioned beliefs about how to work, look, think, or live are optional. Sometimes they are helpful; sometimes not. A simple measure is how they feel in the body: tension, stress, or anxiety signals that a belief may not be serving you, while calm, peace, or increased love toward yourself and others suggests it may be beneficial.

What often drives pain and doubt is like a shadow — a dog that barks but has no bite. Steady practice of READINESS gradually reveals this truth.

Life rarely matches our expectations. We may resist or defend, but over time we see the emptiness of rigid expectations. This slow process opens the way to insight and clarity.

The N-E-S-S Principles

N — Not-Self
Patterns, habits, and unhelpful thoughts are not your essence. They are impermanent, like dandelions or weeds in a garden.

E — Empty
These patterns arise from past conditioning but do not define you. Their apparent "force" depends on engagement — merely noticing them without attachment reveals their emptiness.

S — Suffering
Re-engaging old habits can cause suffering. Observing them without automatic reaction prevents harm and supports steadiness.

S — Subject to Change
All patterns are malleable. Even deeply ingrained habits can shift through consistent, mindful attention.

It is not unusual to wait months or even years before these aspects become visible, so do not strive; understand that this is a gradual process.

Summary

- Not-Self: Patterns are not your essence.
- Empty: They lack inherent reality.
- Suffering: Feeding old habits causes predictable harm.
- Subject to Change: Deep patterns can be reshaped.

Together, these principles guide the gardener to act skillfully and patiently, preserving stability while gradually transforming the garden.

Process in brief:
notice → refrain from reactive engagement → investigate → discern harm → allow insight → pattern weakens → stability is preserved

Step 2: READINESS Summary Table

Principle	Practice / Insight	Gardening Analogy
Recognize	Notice what is not serving you. Self-observation reveals negative reactions in mind, body, and senses that harm your well-being.	Like a gardener noticing which plants serve their vision of an ideal garden and which do not.
Endure & Accept	With calm awareness, observe negative reactions without reacting, suppressing, or feeding them.	Like a gardener watering, fertilizing, and giving sun only to desired plants; unwanted plants are left uncared for.
Discern Danger	Recognize patterns that could harm your well-being. Prune only what interferes with your goals while maintaining overall stability.	Like a gardener knowing that tending unwanted plants will let them spoil the garden.
Investigate	Examine all negative reactions: • Triggers • Maintaining factors (engagement, belief, taking personally) • Perpetuating factors (core stored beliefs) Question whether these beliefs are valid, fit with your experience, benefit your growth or limit you.	Decide what you will keep, what you will let go. Like examining weeds: identifying triggers (water), maintaining factors (pruning), perpetuating factors (seeds). Does the plant support your Garden's vision - whatever that is? Remove attention to the undesired plants- and those plants die off naturally.

Not-Self	Recognize that core beliefs are learned, have causes, and can be unlearned. They are not your essence.	Weeds, dandelions, or unwanted plants are not part of the gardener—they are separate from the garden's identity.
Empty	Conditioning lacks inherent substance; beliefs are like words on a page, empty unless given power.	Mental anchors are like empty soil unless cultivated intentionally.
Subject to Change	All patterns are impermanent and malleable. With reflection and effort, habits and beliefs can be reshaped.	Just as a gardener reshapes the garden, removing or guiding plants over time, habits can be transformed.
Suffering	Continuing to engage with harmful patterns causes predictable harm: anxiety, anger, longing, dissatisfaction.	Weeds left unattended can overtake the garden. By taking agency, the gardener prevents harm and promotes flourishing.

Bringing it Together

- A gardener doesn't fret about weeds; they know these will disappear when the right plants grow.
    - The best gardeners plant gratitude, compassion, joy for others, and goodwill — flowers that benefit both themselves and others at no cost. These will be described in the Endure and Accept section.
- Gardens require patience, observation, discernment, consistency, and persistence.
- A well-tended garden can be enjoyed even when the world outside is uncertain and changing.
- Gardening is both an art and a practice of steady, intentional care—the reward is the garden itself.

Step 3. The Skillful Gardener (Overview)

Step 3 builds on the foundations established in Step 2. While READINESS develops the capacity to recognize experience, endure difficulty, and stop reinforcing unhelpful patterns, Step 3 concerns what becomes possible when insight begins to shape how one lives. For this reason, Step 3 is not relevant until Step 2 is reasonably well established.

At this stage, we move beyond moment-to-moment experience. As understanding of triggers, maintaining factors, and habitual patterns accumulates, insight gradually emerges — a deeper seeing that changes orientation rather than merely informing technique. From this insight arises discernment: the capacity to distinguish what is beneficial from what is not, not as a rule or belief, but as lived understanding. Discernment supports alignment, as choices, values, and life structures begin to reflect what is seen more clearly. From this alignment, agency increases, and action becomes less reactive and more intentional. Over time, this movement supports greater coherence, meaning, and freedom — not as ideals to achieve, but as qualities that emerge from living in closer relationship with reality. This is the basis of an authentic life, shaped by understanding rather than conditioning.

To describe this shift, I use the metaphor of the skillful gardener. The garden represents the whole of one's lived life — inner patterns, relationships, commitments, pace, and direction. The gardener refers to the capacity to care for this life wisely, with patience and perspective, rather than reacting automatically from inherited conditioning. Gardening here does not mean control or perfection, but stewardship: responding to conditions as they are, and supporting what leads to stability and clarity over time.

When doing this work without the ongoing support of a therapist, coach, or suitably grounded guide, you take on the gardener role yourself. In this case, the skillful gardener helps maintain coherence and safety, ensuring that insight is integrated gradually rather than acted out impulsively. External guidance can also serve as an "external gardener," offering perspective and stability when needed. What matters most is that such support is compassionate, steady, and oriented toward clarity rather than control.

Broadly speaking, the capacity of the gardener develops in two stages:

The Procedural Gardener (Step 2)

In the procedural stage, the gardener is developing the basic capacities that allow insight to function at all. Attention is trained to recognize experience, remain present without becoming overwhelmed, and interrupt the reinforcement of unhelpful patterns. At this stage, the gardener is learning how to see clearly and apply READINESS skillfully. The focus remains on stabilization and non-reinforcement, not on shaping life direction.

The Skilful Gardener (Step 3)

As insight accumulates and patterns loosen, a more mature form of guidance becomes possible. The experienced gardener corresponds to Step 3. Here, discernment is more reliable, agency is less driven by old rules or inherited beliefs, and there is greater flexibility in how one engages with life. Insight is no longer something that must be consciously applied — it is increasingly embodied.

At this stage, the gardener may also recognize that the garden itself reflects choices made under earlier constraints. Cultivating coherence may therefore involve revising not only inner reactions, but also the structure, commitments, and direction of one's life. This progression is not about perfection, but about orientation: attention shifts from managing symptoms to living with greater coherence, meaning, and freedom.

In lived terms, the experienced gardener expresses this stewardship through three complementary modes of cultivation:

> - Daily Tending refers to subtle, ongoing adjustments that maintain stability and prevent old patterns from quietly reasserting themselves.
> - Periodic Alignment involves stepping back to review and gently reshape the broader structure of one's life so it reflects emerging clarity, values, and priorities.
> - Over time, this supports Deep Cultivation — a slower, intentional engagement with meaning, values, relationships, and uncertainty. These are not strategies or mandates, but natural expressions of an experienced gardener who can steward insight across time.

The movement from procedural regulation to experienced stewardship can be seen in everyday life. Someone may begin by noticing anxiety, people-pleasing, or self-doubt and learning to stop reinforcing those patterns. Over time, as understanding deepens, they may also question the life structures and identities those patterns once supported — discovering not only how to regulate experience, but how to live more truthfully.

This is the deeper promise of becoming a skillful gardener: not merely reducing distress, but learning to live in alignment with clarity rather than conditioning.

The READINESS Method

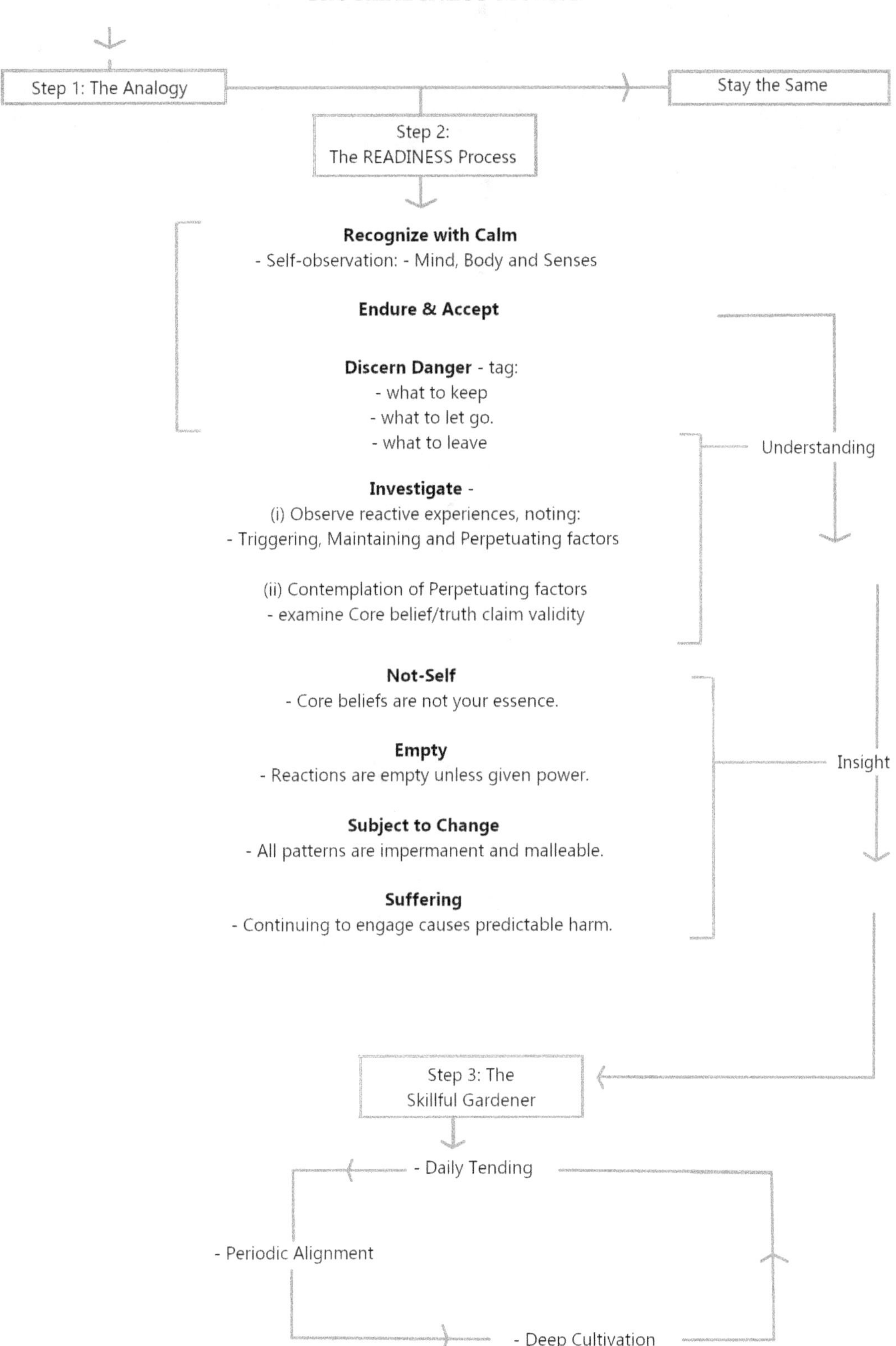

35

Step 2:
Using READINESS

Successful READINESS: Journaling / Planning

Before I start explaining READINESS and you begin using it, I want to discuss how to get the most out of the process. Keeping a dedicated notebook, planner, or journal can be extremely helpful. This journal is a place to record insights, track your practice, and plan how to incorporate the exercises into daily life. Writing things down does more than provide a record — it allows you to clarify your understanding, notice patterns, and see progress over time. It also makes the practice more tangible and portable, so you can reflect even on busy or distracted days.

Throughout this book, I will offer exercises, prompts, and tables that can be directly used in your journal. You don't need anything fancy — a simple notebook is enough. The key is to make the act of journaling part of your READINESS practice, so you can capture insights, notice obstacles, and plan steps for integrating the exercises into everyday life.

How a Journal Helps

- Clarity: Writing down what you observe in body, senses, or mind gives you concrete feedback on your practice.
- Consistency: Planning daily or weekly practice increases follow-through.
- Reflection: Looking back at entries allows you to see growth, notice recurring patterns, and adjust your approach.
- Integration: You can plan how to apply skills like Calm, Recognize, and Endure in practical, real-life situations.
- Example Plan

June

- Week 1: Daily practice of Calm (Mon–Wed) & Presence (Thu–Sun)
- Week 2: Observation of Body/Breathing daily
- Week 3: Observation of Senses daily
- Week 4: Observation of Mind daily

July

- Week 1: Combined Calm and Observation (Body, Senses, Mind) daily
- Week 2: Observation daily at home, and on train to work and back
- Week 3: Start using Recognize at home and out in public
- Week 4: Identify ways to simplify / continue Recognize practice

August

- Week 1: Simplify unnecessary clutter / Recognize
- Week 2: Simplify computer subscriptions / learn free alternatives / Recognize
- Week 3: Cook at home / Recognize
- Week 4: Continue to master cooking at home / Recognize

September

- Week 1: Start Endure with anxiety about being watched / Simplify garage
- Week 2: Endure temptation to correct people in meetings / Reduce sugar intake
- Week 3: Endure nighttime urge to replay old memories / Continue to clean up diet
- Week 4: Endure memories of school friend without trying to change the past / Continue diet improvements

Example Journal Entry

Friday, 27th
Today I noticed a lingering sense that something was wrong — a feeling like a threat of blame or that something might go existentially wrong. At first it felt very real, but I recognized it as a conditioned reaction I had experienced before.

Because I'm familiar with this pattern, I could endure and accept the feeling. I noticed it without getting swept up in it, like a birdwatcher identifying a familiar bird. The sensation was moderately intense and tempting, but I could see it would lead nowhere if I engaged with it.

As I investigated, I realized recent uncertainties and ongoing worries had triggered this feeling. It wasn't about any specific event; it was tied to the core belief that I am not safe. Reminding myself that I am safe and supported helped me stay present and not get caught up in the story. Over time, the feeling naturally passed.

Using READINESS, I reflected that this reaction was not me, had no inherent power, and was subject to change. It was simply a human response. By observing without reacting, I reduced the chance of it returning. I also recognized my need for reassurance and could meet it by grounding myself and avoiding things that make me feel out of control, like certain social media.

This experience reminds me to maintain calm, focus on what genuinely supports my well-being, and continue cultivating awareness over my automatic reactions.

By keeping a journal like this, you not only plan your practice but also create a personal map of your progress. Over time, you can look back and see how calm, presence, and recognition became integrated into daily life — and how small adjustments in focus or environment can make the practice even more effective.

Alternative Table Option – Example Reflection

- Recognize with Calm: Noticed tightness when reading about a friend's wedding.

- Endure / Accept: Allowed the feeling to exist without suppressing it or overthinking. Observed the reaction calmly.

- Discern Danger: Recognized that a similar reaction has occurred before, often linked to feeling "left behind." This could indicate a non-beneficial reaction tied to past beliefs.
  (Note: Beneficial = follow/act on; Neither Beneficial nor Non-beneficial = no mental energy/reaction/action; Non-beneficial = do not react/follow)

- Investigate: Later, in meditation, observed the narrative calmly. The underlying belief is: "Marriage is necessary and I am behind in life." Noted that this belief is inaccurate — I am not behind.
  (Note: triggers, maintaining factors, and perpetuating roots)

- Not-Self: My marital status does not define who I am.

- Empty: The tightness itself has no inherent meaning — allow it to exist without attaching significance.

- Subject to Change: This tightness does not require any action; it may change naturally.

- Suffering: Suppressing the feeling or worrying about marriage would not benefit me. Observing it without judgment is more constructive.

Recognize - Calm Comes First

As you may recall, the first step of READINESS is Recognize with Calm — seeing what is happening in your body, senses, and mind. This is followed by Endure and Accept, when we notice that difficult emotions are present.

There is one skill that greatly increases the chance that these steps will be successful: calm. READINESS is needed because our nervous system often runs tense and reactive, showing up as tight muscles, shallow breathing, adrenaline and cortisol release, and racing thoughts. To see problems clearly — and to sit with them without making them worse — we need to learn how to create calm.

Calm, as a skill on its own, can resolve many problems of reactivity, often without needing to use the full READINESS protocol. It supports observation, prevents automatic reactions, and clarifies perception.

For some people, additional practices such as yoga, gentle movement, or guided hypnosis can further support relaxation and grounding. These are optional, complementary tools that help the body and mind return to a state of safety and ease, making it easier to practice the core READINESS skills.

If you cannot establish a workable level of grounding, consider seeking support from a mental health professional to ensure other factors — such as untreated mood or personality disorders — are appropriately addressed. As outlined in the overview, Recognize works best when calm is established. Here we explore practical ways to create that calm.

Practical Application

Take a moment to reflect:

- When in your life have you felt truly calm?
- What did that calm feel like in your body? Where did you notice it most?

Learning how to create calm, and how to recognize difficult emotions and thoughts, both start with the same practice: gentle observation of the breath. When we tune into the breath and bring soft attention to it, breathing naturally slows and deepens. This helps release tension, soften tightness, and restore a sense of ease. Supportive posture and simple movements — such as gently shaking out tension — can further help the body return to a feeling of safety.

At first, practice creating calm in short, intentional periods at home. Over time, integrate it into daily life. Many skills within READINESS begin as meditation and later become lived skills, including:

- Calming and slowed breathing — sometimes called Shamatha or mindfulness of breathing
- Self-observation of mind, body, and senses — used in Recognize and Endure
- Seeing danger and Investigate — calm contemplation of harm and inquiry into triggers and patterns
- Seeing illusions — observing recurring patterns in conditioning, and exploring their illusory qualities (N.E.S.S in READINESS)

Everything begins with calm. From there, we develop a set of interrelated skills, each supporting the other, all with practical value in helping us release old patterns and relate to experience — and reality itself — in a new way.

Recognize: Calming Meditation - How to

The goal of here is straightforward: relaxation of reactive nrevous system to a calm one.

By focusing on the breath, we gently release tension in the body and mind, letting go of stress, distraction, and passion. Over time, this practice creates ease, tranquillity, and presence. As calm deepens, the background noise of the mind settles, and the habit energy of passion begins to dissolve on its own.

We begin with short, consistent sessions and gradually increase duration. The key is to practice with patience, persistence, and eventually, portability—using the skill throughout daily life, not just in formal sitting.

To do that, we need to master two areas:

1. Physical Technique – Posture and Breathing
2. Mental Technique – Presence, Breath Awareness, Calm, and Equanimity

Let's look at each in turn, starting with posture.

Physical Technique – Posture

In meditation, we adopt an upright posture—not rigid, but steady and dignified. This serves several key purposes:

- The Conditioned Mind often produces self-critical, slouched, deflated postures. Sitting upright counters that energy and asserts confidence.
- An upright pose signals the dignity of a free mind—light, awake, and unburdened.
- Good posture reduces common barriers to practice, such as drowsiness or discomfort.
- A straight spine allows for energy to flow upward, supporting the effort to calm the mind.

Sit in a position that supports this alignment—on a cushion, kneeling bench, or chair. Use the images provided (end of chapter) as a guide. Approach the posture with relaxed curiosity, not as a task you must "get right," but as a gentle support for ease and presence.

✦ ✦ Practice Inquiry ✦ ✦
Sit as you are. Adjust your posture gently:

Let your spine lengthen upward.
Let the shoulders roll back and soften.
Bring a light tension to your core, like you're supporting a sail.

Now pause—what do you notice?
Any subtle mental shift?
Any change in mood or clarity?
(Take 30 seconds just to be upright and aware.)
✦ ✦ ✦ ✦

Physical Technique – Breathing

With posture established, we now turn to the breath—the natural rhythm of life. Breathing is constant, effortless, and always available. It grounds us in the present. Through intentional attention, breath becomes a bridge between body and mind, between scattered thought and grounded awareness.

Diaphragmatic Breathing

In calming, we use diaphragmatic breathing—also called abdominal or belly breathing. This method draws air deeply into the lungs, expanding the belly rather than lifting the chest.

✦ ✦ Practical Application ✦ ✦
- *Place one hand on your chest and one on your belly.*
- *Breathe in slowly. Let the belly rise, while the chest remains mostly still.*
- *Breathe out fully, letting the body soften.*
- *Silently repeat the words:*
"Deep. Abdominal. Slow. Smooth."

This kind of breathing increases oxygen exchange and stimulates the relaxation response. It creates both physical spaciousness and mental ease.
As you inhale, let the breath create openness in your mind and body.
As you exhale, imagine letting go of any tension, self-concern, or striving.
✦ ✦ ✦ ✦

The Goal Is Calm

In calming meditation, you may become aware of thoughts, stories, and mental noise. That's natural. But in this early stage, the goal here is not to analyze or solve these inner movements. Instead, you simply return to the breath.

- Thoughts arise—notice them.
- Don't follow. Don't fight.
- Gently return to breathing.

Apart from connecting to your breathing, and making sure it is deep and relaxed - you can employ additional methods if you need extra help to develop calm. In the early practice, you can use self-hypnosis, or, for others, yoga can help you reach greater calm. However, the goal is still to be able to use calm in day to day life. You can add a hypnotic feel, but adding messages to the out breath like: 'I am releasing tension' or 'with each breath out, I feel more and more relaxed.' Yoga can assist by adding a measure and feedback of your relaxation, when you successfully let tension go, you will see your flexibilty and reach improve and this gives you feedback about what you are doing right.

Make the Practice of Calm Something You Love

One of the most important things you can do is make this practice enjoyable. Find pleasure in breathing and releasing tension. Seek out what is soothing and relieving in each session.

Unlike a medication, drug or external distraction. You won't get "hooked"—but you may fall in love with the peace it brings. So, don't see this a task to get done; That can be a barrier. This practice is one of the few places in life where nothing is demanded, and nothing is missing - enjoy it.

Here, you can simply breathe and be—without judgment, goals, or striving.

In a world full of responsibilities and pressure, this is your invitation to step outside that rhythm. Sit, stand, lean, lie down—whatever your posture, let doing nothing become a source of deep restoration.

✦ ✦ Final Inquiry ✦ ✦
What part of this practice felt kind or relieving to you?
Could you allow yourself to approach meditation not as a task, but as a gift?
• What shifts if this isn't something to perform, but something to enjoy?
• Could you look forward to doing nothing?
✦ ✦ ✦ ✦

Recognize: Increasing Presence

Recall from the overview that Recognise is about noticing reactions without acting. Presence helps make that possible. Presence means being fully here—body and senses—as best you can. It sharpens perception, allowing you to notice when the mind pulls you into rumination or reactivity. Presence is simply meeting reality as it is—awake, alert, and receptive. It can be as simple as going for a walk and connecting to what is seen, heard, felt or sensed.

It also awakens energy: the more you practice, the more naturally attentive and alert you become, and the more you can notice when thoughts and conditioned is pulling you into a trance.

Presence allows you to distinguish what is real from what is reactive. You don't need to "try" to be present; effort often pulls you away. Instead, let go of where you are not and simply arrive where you are. As you continue practicing calm, weave in this layer of presence: let calm make presence possible, and let presence deepen the calm.

✦ ✦ *ACTIVITY (2–3 minutes)* ✦ ✦

Read the script below and try it out.

Being Present Meditation Script.

Find a quiet, comfortable space where you can sit undisturbed. Take your seat, allowing your spine to be upright yet relaxed. Close your eyes gently and take a few slow, smooth breaths, letting your body begin to settle. Now, soften your gaze and take in your surroundings with openness. Notice colors, shapes, textures, and sounds. Let your attention move freely without grasping or resisting. Simply observe.

Focus your attention on a single object, such as a flower, or visualize one clearly. Notice its colors, shapes, structure, stillness, and any subtle movements. Take in its form, its scent, the surrounding air, or sounds nearby. Do not label or interpret—just perceive what is present. Let each impression arise and fade naturally.

Slowly close your eyes again. Recall the space, sensations, and feelings you observed. Let them echo gently in your awareness. Bring attention back to your body and breath. Feel your contact with the floor or cushion. Let the breath ground you— calm, steady, and unforced.

Take a moment to appreciate the clarity of presence you have cultivated. This simple, open awareness—just being here and sensing clearly—is the foundation for Recognizing distress before it gains momentum. It is the first skill of READINESS. When you are ready, gently open your eyes and return to your surroundings, carrying this quiet clarity with you into the next moments of your day.

Recognizing Your Body

As described in the overview, the body is a key domain for Recognise. Here we notice signals early to prevent reactive patterns. Being aware of your body is the first step to noticing stress, tension, and reactivity. The body is both a mirror and a guide: it reflects your mental and emotional states and gives you signals you can act on before they escalate. This chapter combines two foundational skills: breath awareness and body mindfulness. Together, they help you recognize signs of distress and build calm, steady attention.

Breath Awareness

By now you have understood observation of your breathing when cultivating calm - So this is always the Starting point. Breathing awareness settles the body and mind, provides clarity, and gives you a stable reference point to return to when reactivity arises.

Body Mindfulness

Once the mind is anchored in the breath, expand your attention to the body. The body reveals tension, discomfort, posture, and other signals that often appear before your mind fully registers stress or craving.

Exercise – Body Scan (3–5 minutes)

1. Sit or lie comfortably.
2. Slowly bring attention to each part of the body, from head to toe.
3. Notice tension, tightness, heaviness, or ease without judgment.
4. Breathe into areas of tension, allowing them to soften naturally.

Reflection:

- Where do you carry tension most?
- How does your breath change when you release these areas?
- Can you notice subtle physical cues—racing heart, tight jaw, shallow breath—that indicate stress?

Posture and Movement

Posture shapes experience. Slumped, rigid, or tense positions often mirror mental agitation. Smooth, fluid movements reflect ease and presence.

The READINESS Method

Exercise – Posture Awareness (1–2 minutes)

- Sit or stand and notice your usual posture.
- Check shoulders, chest, and spine.
- Gently adjust: lengthen the spine, relax the shoulders, and allow the body to feel supported.

Reflection:

- What does your usual posture tell you about your mental state?
- How does adjusting posture affect your breath, tension, or mood?
- Movement can also support awareness: walking, stretching, or gentle exercise with attention to sensations helps connect mind and body.

Using Body Awareness in Daily Life

Your body provides early warning signs of stress, craving, or reactivity. By noticing these, you can respond instead of reacting.

Exercise – Quick Check-In (1 minute)

1. Pause in daily life.
2. Notice your body: breath, tension, heart rate.
3. Allow the body to soften and return to calm.

Reflection:

- Which physical signals indicate tension for you?
- How can noticing them help you respond rather than react?

Integrating Breath and Body Awareness

By combining breath awareness and body mindfulness, you develop the ability to Recognize distress and reactivity clearly:

- Breath anchors your attention and calms the nervous system.
- Body mindfulness reveals subtle tension, posture, and stress signals.
- Together, they create the foundation for staying present and responding skillfully to challenges.

Being able to notice tension, ragged breathing, or poor posture is the first step in Recognize—seeing what's happening in your body before it escalates into reactivity. This clarity allows you to act with calm, rather than being driven by impulse.

Optional Daily Practice

1. Morning Check-In (2–3 minutes): Sit quietly, notice your breath, then scan your body from head to toe.

2. Movement Awareness (5 minutes): Walk or stretch with full attention on body sensations.

3. Evening Reflection (2–3 minutes): Notice where tension arose today, how your body responded, and any moments when you were able to return to calm.

Recognizing the Senses

Our overview highlighted that our senses can trigger automatic reactions. This section focuses on training yourself to notice those early signals. Our senses—sight, sound, smell, taste, touch, and even thoughts—often signal the first signs of tension, craving, or agitation in the mind and body, because they activate our automatic programs.

For example, we may have a desire to be respected, and noticing someone else receiving respect can trigger an automatic reaction. By practicing awareness of these sensory signals, we build the skill to Recognize what's happening in the body and mind—the first step in the READINESS framework. This practice isn't about suppressing or controlling the senses, but about noticing their pull so we can respond with clarity instead of reacting automatically.

Awareness Exercise: Noticing the Senses
Take a moment to pause. Gently look around or close your eyes.
1. Notice what you can see, hear, smell, taste, or feel in the moment.
2. Observe your thoughts and impulses—what arises automatically?
3. Ask yourself:
* *Which senses are pulling my attention most strongly?*
* *How is my body responding? Tight shoulders, shallow breathing, restlessness?*
This simple check-in is enough to catch small disturbances early, giving you space to stay calm and present.

Managing the Pull of the Senses

Our senses are wired to grab attention—sometimes in helpful ways, sometimes in ways that trigger craving or stress. By noticing their influence, we learn to pause before reacting.

Practice:
* *Recall a recent situation where a sight, sound, smell, taste, touch, or thought triggered a reaction.*
* *Simply label what happened: "That's craving," "That's tension."*
* *Observe the impulse without acting on it.*
* *Notice how the body responds—tight muscles, ragged breathing, posture shifts.*
* *Pause and breathe, letting awareness settle the mind and body.*

Sensory Restraint in Daily Life

You don't need to avoid your senses, but you can respond wisely:

- Stop and notice impulses instead of following them automatically.
- Recognize tension or agitation in the body as a signal.
- Allow yourself to feel it without immediately reacting.
- Return attention to the present moment.

This restraint strengthens self-awareness, helping prevent small disturbances from turning into bigger cycles of stress or craving.

Homework / Reflection

- Notice one situation today where a sense triggered tension or craving.
- Pause, label, and observe.
- How does this awareness change your response?
- What shifts in your body, breathing, or posture when you recognize the signal early?

By practicing in small moments, you train your senses to alert you without controlling you, giving your mind and body more freedom and calm.

Recognizing the Mind

As discussed in the overview, Recognise includes observing mental events. We do this without judgment, simply noticing thoughts, emotions, and intentions. Our mind is always active. Thoughts, intentions, emotions, attachments, and preferences arise constantly. At this stage, the goal is simply to notice them as they occur, without trying to change, judge, or suppress them.

Components of Mind to Observe

- Thoughts: Ideas, judgments, or stories running through your head.
- Intentions: Urges to act, avoid, or do something.
- Emotions: Feelings that arise, such as irritation, excitement, or worry.
- Attachments/Clinging: Desire to hold on to people, outcomes, or ideas.
- Preferences: Likes, dislikes, or neutrality toward experiences.

Observation Activities

1. One-Minute Mind Observation
Close your eyes for one minute and simply notice your mind.
- *Do not try to change it.*
- *Observe whether it is busy, quiet, restless, or calm.*
- *Notice any thoughts, feelings, intentions, or preferences as they arise.*

2. Labeling Exercise
When a mental event arises, silently note it:
- *"Thought about ..."*
- *"Intention to avoid ..."*
Simply observe — no need to act on it.

3. Trigger Reflection
Recall a recent small trigger: an irritation, craving, or distraction.
- *Which components appeared? A thought? An intention? A feeling? A preference?*
- *Notice how they arise and pass without reacting.*

Reflection Prompts

- Which types of mental events do you notice most frequently?
- How does pausing to notice them before reacting feel?
- What mental events can you see with practice that you initially glossed over?
- Can you see them as passing events in your mind rather than commands or truths?

Recognizing Mind – Noticing Tendencies

Once you can notice thoughts, intentions, emotions, attachments, and preferences, the next step is to observe their quality:

- Agreeable: Experiences, urges, or inclinations that feel attractive or pull you toward them.
- Disagreeable: Experiences, urges, or inclinations that feel unpleasant or push you away.
- Neutral: Neither strongly agreeable nor disagreeable — simply present.

✦ ✦ *Reflection* ✦ ✦

- *Pick a thought, intention, or feeling that recently arose. Can you identify whether it was agreeable, disagreeable, or neutral?*
- *How does noticing this quality change the way you relate to it?*
- *Try observing without acting — just see whether the mental event feels agreeable, disagreeable, or neutral.*

At this stage, the focus is pure observation. There's no need to judge, fix, or act on anything. Simply noticing the agreeable or disagreeable quality builds the foundation for understanding patterns in your mind and responding wisely in later stages of practice.

Summarizing Recognize With Calm

Bringing together calm and recognition, we practice in body, senses, and mind, as mapped in the overview. We have learned our first and most fundamental skills: Calm and Recognition. Let's bring them together.

Calm is your first step whenever you notice tension or unrest in your nervous system. Before you try to observe yourself, switch on Calm:

- Connect to your breath
- Deepen it
- Release tension in the body
- Slow down and settle

Recognize is what comes next. Use Calm as your foundation, then notice in this order:

1. Breath and body – sense what is present in the body
2. Senses – see what is pulling your attention or stirring reactions
3. Mind – observe thoughts, intentions, emotions, and preferences

Let it all flow together like a wave of calm observation, noticing without pushing, pulling, or judging.

What To Do:

Practice each practice until you have a well rounded Recognize skill that you can perform anywhere and at anytime:

- Calming with observation of breathing
- Recognizing and releasing body tension
- Noticing triggering of the senses with calmness
- Noticing movements in the mind - visualisations, images, sensations, stories, thoughts and so on.

It is hard for me to say how many times and how regularly you need to do these skills, but the important thing is that you looking at bringing it into daily life. Once you have the basics, and remember to use it in your day, it quickly becomes second nature.

Activities: Practice each domain, then document your observations in a journal or table (see Successful READINESS: Journalling / Planning).

Endure and Accept - Introduction

Endure and Accept builds on Recognise: once calm observation is established, we can allow reactions to arise without acting, suppressing, or forcing them. The goal is to strengthen your capacity to sit with experiences safely, gaining insight over time.

Preparing for Endure and Accept
Before practicing endurance, it helps to create mental space by reducing unnecessary stressors. Simplification supports endurance by removing avoidable triggers, making reactions easier to observe. Specific strategies for simplification will follow in the next section.

Core Practice - When reactive urges arise:

1. Notice them.
2. Allow them to be present.
3. Observe with curiosity, without feeding, suppressing, or acting on them.

Key Points:

- Endure and Accept is not suppression or denial.
- Acceptance does not mean something is good, fair, or desirable — it simply exists.
- Calm observation lets reactions soften, fade, or become clearer over time.

Practical Examples:

- A memory of a co-worker who caused frustration arises → notice the tension without following the story.
- Waking with dread → observe the feeling calmly, acknowledging it without letting it dictate your actions.
- Sharing an opinion that leads to regret → notice the reaction, allow it to be present, then return to the present moment.

Building Endurance Muscles:

- Like exercising a muscle, endurance grows with repeated practice.
- Notice which "plants" (patterns) in your mental garden need attention, and which can be left alone.

- Over time, Endure and Accept becomes easier, even during discomfort.

✦ ✦ *Reflection* ✦ ✦
Consider your own "garden": which mental patterns do you already know you want to observe without reacting?
Example: "I overthink scenarios like 'what if this goes wrong?'"
✦ ✦ ✦ ✦

Activities: Use Recognize with calm, then Endure and Accept. Journal or table your observations (see Successful READINESS: Journalling / Planning).

Endure and Accept: Why Simplification?

Endurance becomes easier when the mind isn't overloaded with unnecessary stressors. Simplifying life reduces triggers, giving you the mental space to observe reactions calmly.

Ways to Simplify

1. Material and Financial:

- Let go of things that demand constant attention or maintenance.
- Reduce subscriptions, memberships, or unnecessary costs.
- Choose simpler, affordable alternatives that meet real needs.

2. Personal Habits:

- Replace unsustainable routines with manageable ones.
- Reduce habits, addictions, or behaviors that drain energy or peace of mind.
- Maintain personal space and boundaries; avoid unnecessary chaos.

3. Mental Noise:

- Limit emotionally charged or excessive information.
- Be selective with social media and news.
- Focus only on what is within your control.

4. Time and Commitments:

- Say no to roles or expectations that don't align with your values.
- Reclaim time for rest, reflection, and meaningful connections.

Distinguishing Necessary vs. Unnecessary

Over time, notice what genuinely supports clarity and wellbeing versus what carries hidden costs. Examples of necessary supports:

- Food, shelter, safety, healthcare
- Rest, reflection, and creative activity
- Trustworthy relationships
- Freedom to pursue meaningful goals

Ongoing Question for Practice: Does this activity or commitment support calm, clarity, and insight, or does it add unnecessary stress?

Endure and Accept: Safety & Stability

Endure and Accept builds on Recognise: before practicing, you should already be able to create calm and observe reactions safely. If grounding or self-awareness is not yet stable, see the guidance in the Recognise chapter and consider professional support.

Situations suitable for self-practice:

- The triggering situation is over, or there is no immediate crisis.
- Acting on thoughts or emotions would not create risk to yourself or others.
- Reactions are familiar, manageable, and previously experienced.

Situations requiring professional support:

Do not attempt Endure and Accept alone if you experience:

- Severe trauma, emotional instability, or EUPD / borderline-type patterns
- Psychotic episodes or dissociation
- Mood disorders with active crisis or suicidal thoughts
- High-risk behaviors or poor judgment
- Situations where safety — your own or others' — is compromised

Enduring and accepting reactions is not suppression or self-abandonment. This practice is meant for manageable experiences, not to tolerate dangerous situations or neglect mental health needs.

Practical Example Table

Situation	Reaction	Can I Manage?	Suggested Action
Memory of co-worker sabotage	Annoyance	Yes	Notice sensation, breathe, observe without following the story
Intense, unfamiliar panic	Overwhelming urge to act	No	Use calming techniques, seek support, maintain safety, consider professional guidance

When to Proceed:

- Crisis or safety issues are resolved
- Support systems are in place if needed
- You have a baseline sense of calm and self-awareness

Reminder: Endure and Accept is safe and useful only when your foundation is stable. For high-risk situations, severe personality patterns, or intense unfamiliar reactions, work with a trained professional first.

Endure and Accept: How It's Done

Check Your Skills First

Before practicing, ensure you can:

- Bring calm into your system (Recognise)
- Observe reactivity without immediately acting
- Reduce unnecessary triggers through simplification
- Maintain independence, insight, and motivation

Once these conditions are met, Endure and Accept can happen naturally, without force.

Step-by-Step Practice

1. Notice the Reaction

   - When a thought, memory, or bodily sensation arises, simply recognize it.
   - Name it mentally if helpful ("tension," "dread," "irritation").

2. Allow It to Be Present

   - Let the experience exist without trying to push it away or control it.
   - Avoid suppressing or following the urge.

3. Observe With Curiosity

   - Pay attention to physical sensations, emotions, or mental images.
   - Note patterns without judgment or personalizing.

4. Step Back From the Story

   - Focus on the direct experience, not the narrative your mind creates.
   - Breath or posture can help anchor awareness.

5. Let It Pass in Its Own Time

   - Some reactions fade quickly, others require repeated observation.
   - Endurance strengthens with practice; over time, reactions become easier to observe calmly.

Practical Example

David notices a familiar "high-strung" feeling in the morning. He:

- Focuses on breath, calming posture.
- Observes neck tension and shallow breathing.
- Notices mental images spinning without following them.
- Reminds himself to only observe, not resist or act.
- Gradually, the sensation fades; he notes he doesn't fully understand it yet but recognizes it is manageable.

Reflection & Integration

- Identify recurring "plants" in your mental garden: patterns or reactions you will observe without feeding.
- Use repeated observation to build confidence and insight.
- Investigation and deeper understanding can follow once endurance is established.

Summary

Endure and Accept is practical, skill-based, and progressive:

- Observe, allow, and stay present.
- Avoid suppressing or engaging the reaction.
- Build endurance gradually, using calm and simplification to support practice.
- Over time, insight emerges naturally.

Discern Danger

As introduced in the overview, "Discern Danger" is a step in the READINESS process for recognizing patterns we have already tagged through observation. Here, we explore how to apply this discernment in practice.

Ignoring problematic patterns allows them to grow, which can harm our well-being. At the same time, everything our senses, body, and mind do is conditioned. We cannot—and should not—try to apply READINESS to everything. Instead, we focus on identifying reactions that are beneficial, neutral, or non-beneficial. This process involves careful observation, reflection, and investigation.

Example Of Discernment In Action:

- Annoyance might initially seem clearly non-beneficial. However, by observing and investigating the context, we may discover that our irritation signals a violated boundary, such as being treated without respect by a close partner. In this case, the reaction serves us—it flags something important and can guide a wise response.

After discernment, we can make informed choices about what to cultivate, remain neutral toward, and avoid feeding. For example:

Beneficial / Cultivate
- What: Gratitude. Why: Focusing on what I have improves well-being and perspective.

Neutral
- What: Work. Why: Necessary to cover costs; neither wholly positive nor negative.

Non-beneficial
- What: Pursuit of Power / Status. Why: Increases stress without lasting benefit; simpler choices lead to more contentment.

Guiding Principles For Discern Danger:

- Respect stability: Our mind is conditioned, and abrupt or excessive change can destabilize us. Gradual, thoughtful adjustments maintain a sense of self and responsibility to others.

- Observe and reflect: Contemplate what truly supports your well-being. Adjust patterns that hinder your aims, maintain what works, and avoid changes that feel forced or superficial.

- Balance wisdom and agency: Use discernment to act in alignment with your own values and vision, rather than inherited conditioning.

Additional Examples:

- Religion may provide deeply beneficial patterns (e.g., compassion, love) but also carry beliefs that generate guilt or shame. Discernment allows us to retain what supports us and release what no longer serves, applying READINESS to emotions like guilt or anxiety with clarity and calm.

- As in a garden metaphor: a large oak tree provides stability; you may selectively prune branches to let in light but do not remove the tree entirely. Similarly, retain helpful patterns, adjust only what genuinely hinders, and maintain overall balance.

By practicing Discern Danger, we gradually develop the ability to recognize, assess, and wisely respond to patterns, cultivating a mental "garden" that supports well-being, stability, and agency.

Building Understanding of the 'Beneficial'

Earlier, we explored how the question of what is "beneficial" is not always straightforward, and how our assumptions about it can shift as we gain insight. For the purpose of DISCERN DANGER, we use a simple orientation: something is beneficial when it does not require us to abandon ourselves — meaning it preserves basic self-respect, compassion, and understanding — while also not causing unnecessary harm to others. It also recognizes that living for others' approval or comfort is not the same as living wisely; we cannot keep everyone happy without losing ourselves.

This working understanding is enough for now. The deeper cultivation of the beneficial comes later. When you feel ready, move to Step 3: Cultivating the Beneficial and begin contemplating what you see as truly beneficial in your own life. Contemplation may be done meditatively, or anytime the mind is calm and non-reactive enough to look with even-mindedness.

Activities: If there are early, easy experiences you can clearly discern as non-beneficial ("bad plants"), journal or table your observations.

Investigate - Introduction

Investigation is the next essential skill. It has two key components: Investigation and Contemplation. These can be done in quiet calm reflection, or as meditation.

Investigation

We begin by asking: "What am I feeling?" When a strong emotion—such as angst—is recognized, we first Endure and Accept it. We notice the feeling and apply Discerning as Danger.

Next, we investigate the distress by exploring three areas:

1. Observable triggers – What sparks the pattern?
   Example: Seeing a crowd.

2. Maintaining factors – What habits or actions sustain the reaction?
   Example: Imagining people laughing at me.

3. Perpetuating factors – What underlying beliefs fuel the pattern?
   Example: "I'm awkward."

Through this process, we begin to see the responsible conditioning and its effects. We observe how old conditioning causes new situations to go wrong for us. This exploration forms the basis for deeper understanding.

Contemplation

Once we identify the core belief(s) that trigger distress, we ask: "Is this belief truly to my benefit? Do I want this plant in my garden?"

Contemplation allows us to process old learning with calm and careful reflection, reaching a thorough understanding and a satisfactory decision. Using Socratic questioning and curiosity, we test each belief: Does it fit with reason? With our wishes for life?

Through this process, we develop clear discernment. When we fully understand our decision and doubts are resolved, we can confidently apply READINESS to all future reactions of this kind. Over time, the emotional reaction weakens, and the original core belief loses its power—or may even fade entirely.

Discernment creates vision and alignment. As old, unhelpful truths drop away, we gain the space to decide what will take their place. This is where we establish new values, identify what gives life meaning, and author what would make our life worthwhile—even if it is not always easy.

This becomes our plan for a new garden. We use it to guide our alignment and refine our investigation and discernment, ensuring that our choices consistently align with our vision.

Investigate - Procedural Step

Here's how procedural investigation works. Note: At first, practice this as a meditation at home, in a safe and calm environment. As your skill improves, you can extend it to other situations, depending on your comfort and confidence.

Context in READINESS:

1. Recognize – "What am I feeling?"
   Example: I notice I'm not calm. My body and breathing are tense, I cannot look people in the eye, and my mind is anxious.

2. Endure and Accept
   I acknowledge the anxiety. This is a feeling I have not investigated before.

3. Discern Danger
   The anxiety feels unhelpful, like a signal of danger. I check whether I am calm and grounded enough to investigate. If not, I may wait until I am home, supported, or feeling safe.

4. Investigate (Procedural)

   • Observe triggers: What sparks this pattern?
   • Understand maintaining factors: What habits or actions sustain it?

   • Identify perpetuating factors: What beliefs underlie it?

The table below provides guidance with questions to ask and contemplate for each stage.

Trigger	Maintaining factors	Perpetuating factors
Purpose / Things to Consider		
Identify what sets off the pattern. Consider recent sense data: sights, sounds, tastes. Notice automatic reactions: memories, flashbacks, sensations of being unsafe.	See what feeds and sustains the reaction. Look for preferences (like/dislike) and identification (ownership, making it personal, mental stories).	Identify the seed—the underlying beliefs, ideas held as "true," values (should, shouldn't, could, would), and desires to rewrite reality (fantasies, imagined alternatives).

Questions to Ask		
How did this start? Did a sight, sound, or smell trigger a memory or feeling?	Do I have a strong preference about this (want/don't want, fight or flight)? Am I personalizing this? Do I feel I must act, worry, or think about it more?	Why do I think this is relevant to me? What do I believe is wrong or correct here? What makes me feel I should act now? Can I trace the root?

Example		
I walked in last to the meeting, and everyone turns to look—they all look amused.	I don't like it, I feel in the spotlight. I make it about me: "They must be talking about me; they don't like my new haircut."	I think: "People shouldn't be so rude," "Why does everyone stare all the time?" I imagine telling them to stop being rude and to respect me. I have a core belief that I must be approved of to be safe. Strong dislike triggers my ego, making me jump to conclusions and personalize events.

Actions / Reflections		
Endure and accept the sights/triggers.	Endure and accept the preference and identification. Observe with calmness.	Endure and accept—observe desires and wishes without acting on them.

What You Learn / Summarize Insights From Your Investigation.
I notice that old conditioning—such as the belief that i must be approved to feel safe—drives automatic reactions, like personalizing situations and jumping to conclusions. Observing these reactions calmly allows me to see their source and gradually reduce their power. I will practice noticing triggers and underlying beliefs as they arise, enduring discomfort without reacting. over time, I will replace unhelpful patterns with responses aligned with my values and vision.

In this example, a seemingly "random" sense of anxiety now makes complete sense: my learned belief, "I must be liked to be safe," sits in my garden like a seed, ready to sprout and cause the same problem repeatedly. When I see people turn my way, that seed is triggered. My preference for the feeling to stop immediately draws me in, and I create a story—that they are thinking about me—even though this story is incorrect. By observing and contemplating what is happening, I can see the process clearly. If I truly believe I must be liked to be safe, of course I would agonize about it.

Immediate Healing

Healing begins immediately. Using READINESS, I stay calm, breathe deeply, and release tension. My Endurance and Acceptance allow me to cope long enough to see the event clearly. Over time, I can notice triggers, the stories I tell, and false conclusions. I can label this plant as "Danger" because I have discerned it well. I neither act on the story nor suppress it; I simply observe it.

READINESS is on your side. Conditioned reactions are like robots: sometimes helpful, sometimes not. The process gives me agency, seeing me as worthy of love, understanding, and compassion. It is kind, supportive, and non-threatening. If tired, I can pause; if motivated, I can observe more. It cultivates wise mind: "You're being hard on yourself. You are okay. You can be strong. You will get through this."

Why Investigation is Empowering

The maintaining factors—the ways we participate in the cycle—are subtle but crucial. Recognizing how I feed the seed, personalize events, and create stories may feel shocking. But this is excellent news: when I clearly see these patterns, I know exactly what to do. Using READINESS on identification and participation prevents me from propping up the cycle, weakening it over time.

Investigation Builds Insight

By breaking the cycle into parts, I begin to see the illusions created by conditioned beliefs. My belief that "things are like this" triggers the anxiety, my involvement, and the repeating cycle. Now, having understood it, I can plan to stop the seed from sprouting in the future, which we explore in Contemplation.

When experiences arise, follow R, E, A, D. In Investigate, note the Trigger, Maintaining Factors, and Perpetuating Roots. Record your observations in a journal or table (see Successful READINESS: Journaling / Planning).

Investigate - Contemplative Step

We now move into Contemplation, which completes the Investigation step—the "I" in the READINESS framework.

Up to this point, we have:

- Recognized our reaction,
- Endured it without avoidance,
- Accepted it as it is, and
- Discerned potential danger in how we have been responding.

In the previous chapter, we used procedural investigation to examine the trigger, the maintaining factors, and the perpetuating factors, tracing the reaction back to an underlying core belief.

Having identified this belief, we now shift from observing how the reaction functions to contemplating whether the belief itself is worth keeping.

The Purpose of Contemplation

Contemplation uses general contemplative questions, supported by a structured table, to explore a core belief thoroughly and calmly. The aim is not to force change, argue with the belief, or replace it prematurely, but to understand it clearly enough to make an informed decision.

This process is grounded in Socratic questioning. It respects the individual's autonomy:

- A person may decide a belief is non-beneficial or harmful,
- They may decide it is neutral, or
- They may decide it is something they wish to retain.

If a belief is seen clearly and judged to be non-beneficial, the READINESS framework provides gentle, gradual ways of loosening identification with it, rather than attacking or suppressing it.

Why Contemplation Works

Because this method is rational, systematic, and experiential, it is effective at addressing core beliefs without threat. As beliefs are examined and clarified:

- Identification with them weakens,
- Triggers lose intensity, and
- Our capacity to remain present with strong emotion increases.

Over time, repeated contemplation reveals the constructed nature of conditioning and the cascading effects it produces—insights that will be explored more deeply in later chapters.

General Contemplative Questions

Use the following questions to explore the core belief slowly and honestly:

- Why does this belief exist?
- Where did I learn it?
- Who taught me this belief, and do they represent my values now?
- Does this belief align with my vision for my life?
- In what ways does this belief reduce compassion toward myself or others?
- When I hold this belief, what is it trying to make me avoid or distract me from?
- What part of myself is being denied or constrained by this belief?
- What expectations does this belief create that I could let go of?
- How is this belief attempting to control people or situations I cannot control?
- Does it offer real control—or only the illusion of control?

Additional Contemplative Frameworks

After working through the general questions, it can be helpful to reflect using a few additional lenses, including:

- The self-evident facts of life (change, aging, sickness, death, limitation),
- The subjective and learned nature of core beliefs, and
- Whether the belief is genuinely beneficial or merely familiar.

The accompanying tables provide example questions and brief sample reflections for each framework, helping translate contemplation into practical inquiry. In the Tables I use an Example Core Belief: 'A life without success is worthless'.

Self-Evident Facts		
Change Will Happen.	*Aging And Sickness Are Real.*	*Death Is Real.*
- How will change affect this core belief? - What conditions could change that would affect this? - How much control do I really have, and how much is out of my control?	- How would sickness or aging affect this core belief?	- How does death affect this core belief?
Application to Example:		
You could be successful, and that success could be taken away—your business could fail, for example.	If I were terminally ill, would my success still feel important?	If I only live once, is this success truly how I want to spend my life?

Subjectivity (Does Everyone Agree, Or Can Some People Live Without This Belief?)		
Is It Important To All People?	*Is It Universally True?*	*Who Are The People For Whom This Does Not Matter?*
Does everyone in the world hold this to be important? Why is it that so people do not? Can it be okay if people don't act on, think about and worry about this?	Is this belief true at all times - in what ways is it situation dependent? Was this belief always important to people? In what ways was life better before this belief?	Are there people who are not worried about this issue? In what ways does this benefit them? What would happen if I cared less about this?
Application to Example:		
Some people are not worried about success. There are people who create, write journals, or compose poems that are never published, never make money, and are not praised. Success can bring new problems—you have to maintain it and worry about your achievements.	If I had only one week to live, the success of my project or business might not feel important anymore. There was a time when the term "success" didn't exist; survival was the focus, and people didn't think about achievements in the same way. In the past, survival could be achieved, making success a more abstract concept.	Some parents, monks, spiritual practitioners, or ordinary people don't focus on success at all. Not thinking about success can allow for more time, space, calm, and peacefulness. If I let go, I might not need that new refinance. By simplifying, I can live comfortably on my current income and past achievements.

Beneficial Or Not?		
Worth Your Well-Being? (Does It Benefit You?)	*Treat Others as You Would Expect (Making a Better World)*	*Gentleness, Cooperation, and Sharing (Making a Better World)*
Is this core belief worth sacrificing your well-being, whether it be physical, mental, or emotional? Is this belief of value and for the well-being of others?	What happens if this belief is applied to me? Does it respect my well-being, or override it? Would I consent to being on the receiving end of this behaviour?	Would a gentle, kind, or deeply compassionate person see this view as beneficial? Would those who value kindness, mutual support, and human well-being see this view as supportive of cooperation and building a better world?
Application to Example		
Pursuing success at the cost of sleep, health, or peace of mind often leads to burnout and strain, undermining the very stability needed to live well. When success is prioritised above all else, it can foster competition, pressure, or neglect of others' needs, rather than care, cooperation, or mutual well-being.	When this belief is applied to me, I am valued mainly for outcomes and achievement. This often places pressure above well-being and treats rest, limits, and humanity as secondary. From that position, I would not freely consent to being on the receiving end of this behaviour.	A gentle or deeply compassionate person would likely see this view as limited or problematic when held as a priority, as it tends to place achievement above care. Likewise, those who value kindness, mutual support, and human well-being would see it as weak support for cooperation and for building a better world, unless it is clearly subordinate to compassion and care.

After Contemplation - Tag And Release

After identifying the root cause, tag it as Beneficial, Non-beneficial, or Neutral/Leave Alone. This classification becomes useful later in Discern Danger, so when the pattern returns you can follow the action you've already decided. In your journal— or in memory if you don't keep one— track the following:

- Dangerous vs. Beneficial Emotions: Notice which emotional states are expressions of old, non-beneficial conditioning and therefore potentially harmful, versus emotions that are constructive and beneficial—for example, feelings that signal it may be time to change a stressful job or leave a dysfunctional relationship.

- Normal and Necessary States: Recognize emotions that are natural parts of life, like boredom at a repetitive job, the desire to go home after a long day, or the tension of responsibility that comes with being a good parent. These are not part of the READINESS process.

- What to Cultivate: Informed by Investigation, identify the thoughts, behaviors, and emotional habits you want to encourage because they genuinely benefit you.

The table below provides an example. Collecting this kind of information shapes the Competent Gardener you are becoming. It's this experienced, insightful self who decides how your new internal "garden" should grow and who asks the most important question: "What does a good life look like?"

Contemplation Is Not Just for Old Conditioning

Contemplation also tests new values. As you clear old conditioning— letting go of things like fame, academic titles, money worship, or other attachments—you will notice an opening: more space, energy, and time. Dropping a famous project, a multi-year program, debt repayment, or a business idea frees up options. Now you can ask: What takes their place?

For example, you might decide that a new value is: "To explore new places and dedicate my energy to projects where I help others." Contemplation is for this too. Use the General Contemplative Questions and frameworks, because even beneficial values have potential challenges. You may face criticism, skepticism from friends, or doubts about whether you're making the "right" choices.

Ultimately, the person who must be satisfied with your values is you. Contemplation helps you assess whether your chosen path truly aligns with your well-being and priorities, giving you clarity, confidence, and direction.

Example Table:

Cultivate	*To Leave (Necessary)*	*To Reduce (Dangerous):* **Use READINESS for** *experiences such as:*
- Openness - Understanding - Room for Paradox - Acceptance of life's problems - Compassion – noticing opportunities to help others - Sharing wisdom and skills - Bringing the sense of "vast peace" from meditation into daily life, because it enhances well-being	- Money, work, responsibility, and reputation are sometimes necessary.	- Feeling superior or "better than" others - Being prideful about achievements - Wanting more power within your organization - Worrying excessively - Fear of death - Impatience, suspicion, ill will, or prejudging others - Clinging to doctrines, getting tribal, or following the bandwagon - Focusing on strength or physical vanity rather than overall wellness

Activities: When you recognize a Core Belief or Truth Claim, journal or table your observations. Note your discernment about whether it is Beneficial, Non-beneficial, or Neutral (see Successful READINESS: Journaling / Planning).

Investigate - Conclusion

Investigation brings the automatic processes of old, learned habits into the light, allowing us to decide whether they are habits we wish to continue. By combining procedural gardener investigation with thoughtful contemplation, we gain both clarity and agency over our conditioned responses.

Procedural investigation teaches us to break emotional patterns down into triggers, maintaining factors, and perpetuating beliefs. By observing each layer calmly and without judgment, we see how old conditioning drives automatic reactions. This insight is empowering: it shows us exactly where we participate in our own cycles of distress and where we can intervene.

Contemplation completes the process. By carefully examining the core beliefs that underlie our reactions, we ask whether they truly serve our well-being and align with our values. Through Socratic questioning, reflection on life's realities, and consideration of a belief's impact on ourselves and others, we learn to discern which beliefs are worth cultivating, which may be necessary but limited, and which are ready to be let go.

This process is gentle and self-supportive. It does not attack or suppress old patterns, but allows insight to arise naturally, creating space for deliberate, values-aligned choices.

In the next chapter, we explore how continued practice of READINESS builds toward freedom. As calm becomes more stable, involvement in old habits reduces, and their origins become clearer, we naturally confirm our intention not to perpetuate these cycles. This leads to the final aspect of READINESS: the realization that old automatic beliefs are not us, are empty of inherent power, and are subject to change. When clung to, they reliably lead to suffering and distress—and seeing this clearly cements our commitment to change.

Insights gained through investigation are important, so take time to journal what you learn. In a later chapter, we build on this understanding by turning toward a deeper question: What should a good life look like? A life guided by investigation naturally moves toward maximizing what benefits us while minimizing what causes unnecessary distress.

Ultimately, investigation is about reclaiming agency and consciously designing our internal "garden."

N.E.S.S - Completing READINESS

The last four letters of READINESS build on the insights from Investigation: all mental reactions exist for a reason, but today they are optional and don't define who we are. Recognizing this allows us to Endure and Accept more easily.

Step 1: N — Not Myself

Automatic reactions, emotions, and learned habits are not your true self. They are patterns shaped by past experience and conditioning. Observing them without identifying or acting on them gives space to choose a deliberate response.

Exercise:

1. Notice a recurring reaction.
2. Acknowledge it as a pattern, not a command.
3. Reflect: "This is a learned reaction from the past. I can respond differently now."

Example:
Thought: "I need to do something to stay safe."
Insight: Recognize this as the voice of a past self. You can acknowledge it, thank it for its effort, and choose a calmer, deliberate response.

Step 2: E — Empty of Inherent Power

Emotions and urges may feel intense, but their force depends on engagement. By noticing them without automatic reaction, we see they have no independent authority.

Exercise:

- When an emotion arises, simply observe it and label it.
- Ask: "Does this have power if I don't feed it?"
- Notice how its intensity shifts when left unattended.

Example:
Anxiety feels urgent, but it only drives action if you engage with it. Observing without acting reveals its emptiness.

Step 3: S — Subject to Change

All thoughts, feelings, and habits are impermanent. Recognizing their mutability allows you to weaken entrenched patterns. Interrupting even a single step in a habitual loop can transform it.

Exercise:

- Identify a habitual reaction.
- Track its rise and fall over time.
- Notice how skipping a step in the cycle changes the outcome.

Example:
"I feel the urge to react angrily. If I pause and breathe, this urge fades rather than taking control."

Step 4: S — Suffering and Distress

Engaging with unhelpful beliefs or automatic reactions prolongs stress. Observing clearly and choosing whether to act reduces unnecessary suffering and restores calm.

Exercise:

- When a familiar reaction arises, ask:

1. How is this not truly me?
2. How empty is it — if I leave it, how long before it fades?
3. How subject to change is it — will it persist if I don't feed it?
4. Is acting on it worth the suffering it creates?

- Apply these reflections to redirect attention, allow the feeling to pass, or take deliberate action aligned with your values.

    Example:
    Thought: "I must act to prevent harm."
    Insight: Engaging perpetuates worry. Choosing not to feed it restores calm and clarity.

Step 5: Experiencing Release (The Penny Drop)

Activity:
This step combines noticing, reflection, and actual letting go. It may take time, and some patterns may need repeated attention.

1. As thoughts, emotions, or urges appear, recognize them as empty, changeable, optional, and not part of your identity.
2. Sit with this recognition fully. Breathe and observe without judgment.
3. When the understanding settles — the "aha" moment — give yourself permission to release it.
4. Sense the old belief, expectation, or reactive urge loosening its grip, leaving space for calm and deliberate choice.
5. Repeat as needed; some patterns require multiple encounters before they feel fully optional.

Example:

A recurring worry arises: "I must fix this problem to be safe."

- Observe: it's a learned reaction, not a fixed truth.
- Notice it is empty, changeable, and not part of your core identity.
- Sit with this understanding and allow yourself to release the urge to act automatically.

Outcome:
Over time, practicing in this way strengthens your ability to step back from automatic patterns, reclaim agency, and respond with clarity, calm, and deliberate choice. Old patterns gradually lose their automatic hold, creating inner space for intentional living.

Step 3:
The Skillful Gardener:

'What Should a Good Life Look Like?'

The Skillful Gardener - Introduction

Before engaging in Step 3, it's important to remember that this stage depends on the work of Step 2—the Procedural Gardener. Using READINESS to Recognize, Endure, Accept, and Investigate reactions provides the stability, insight, and calm necessary to safely take responsibility for shaping your life.

Step 2 is the foundation: it trains attention, metacognition, and emotional regulation. Step 3—the Experienced Gardener—builds on this foundation, guiding not just reactions but the overall direction, structure, and coherence of your inner garden and your life. Without the procedural work in place, authorship may feel overwhelming or destabilizing.

From Understanding to Authorship

Pause and reflect for a moment:
Who decided what your life should look like? Was it truly you—or did you inherit a script? Even when you succeeded, anxiety and exhaustion often followed. At some point, you may realize that you have been wandering inside a labyrinth—moving from task to task—without stepping back to see the structure you are in. At some point, you may find yourself saying:
"I will decide—not them."

Up to this point, your work has focused on learning to see clearly and to relate differently to what arises. You have practiced noticing patterns, staying present with difficulty, and understanding how certain reactions are conditioned and maintained. This has already changed your relationship to your inner life.

Step 3 marks a shift. Here, the emphasis moves from working with what appears to taking responsibility for how the garden is shaped over time. This is not a rejection of the earlier steps, but their natural maturation. The stability and insight developed through READINESS now become the basis for conscious guidance rather than reactive management.

Many people notice a quiet but significant realization:
"I don't have to keep living according to inherited scripts."

Not scripts enforced by others alone, but those absorbed unconsciously —ideas about success, identity, worth, pace, or meaning. When these loosen, a new question appears:
What should a good life look like—for me?

This question does not require a final answer. It requires orientation. Becoming a skillful gardener means beginning to live from discernment rather than habit, from alignment rather than pressure. It is the moment where insight turns into authorship: where you are no longer only regulating distress, but consciously shaping how you live, choose, relate, and engage with uncertainty.

Importantly, this does not mean striving to design a perfect life. Life remains uncertain, limited, and unfinished. The task here is not control, but stewardship—learning how to guide the garden with care, realism, and flexibility, even when clarity is partial.

In Step 3, the gardener begins to work at three complementary levels:

- Daily Tending — how you respond to what arises moment by moment, preventing old patterns from being unconsciously reinforced.

- Periodic Alignment — how you gently adjust the structure, pace, and direction of your life when misalignment becomes visible.

- Deep Cultivation — how you learn to hold meaning, values, uncertainty, and paradox without collapsing into fear, rigidity, or avoidance.

Together, these are not separate practices, but expressions of the same capacity: the ability to live deliberately without needing certainty, perfection, or external validation.

The chapters that follow explore these dimensions in practical terms. They are not instructions for becoming someone else, but supports for becoming more fully responsible for the garden you are already tending—and for learning how to do so with increasing clarity, calm, and freedom.

The Skillful Gardener - Process

Step 3 moves insight into intentional action. The gardener shifts from observing patterns to actively shaping the garden. This is not control or perfection, but deliberate stewardship: responding to life with clarity, patience, and skill.

The practice unfolds across three complementary levels:

1. Daily Tending — Subtle Reinforcement

Daily tending focuses on small, precise adjustments, maintaining calm and preventing old patterns from reasserting themselves.

Key points:

- Let go of what is non-beneficial
- Reinforce what is beneficial
- Leave what is necessary untouched

Observation and gentle adjustment take priority over striving. Each day, notice where attention, energy, and habits create alignment or friction, and make subtle corrections.

2. Periodic Alignment — Gentle Inclining

Periodic alignment examines the broader structure of life, ensuring the garden reflects your values and priorities.

Focus areas include:

- Freeing up space or time that no longer supports intentions
- Releasing unnecessary commitments or attachments
- Adjusting pace, boundaries, or priorities

This allows the garden to shift naturally toward coherence, without forcing outcomes.

3. Deep Cultivation — Intentional Development

Once daily and periodic practices are established, deep cultivation involves exploring meaning, values, relationships, and uncertainty. It is not problem-solving, but observing, reflecting, and cultivating alignment over time. This is where insight translates into intentional living.

8 Core Areas of Cultivation — A Roadmap

As you move into deeper work, the gardener can focus on eight domains, each explored in subsequent chapters:

Area	Focus
- Grounding of Lived Meaning	- Sense alignment with values and narrative
- Discernment of the Beneficial	- Distinguish what serves versus what hinders
- Spiritual Grounding	- Orient toward higher principles provisionally
- Relational Grounding	- Navigate solitude, intimacy, and community
- Skillful Living	- Calm, flexibility, inward mastery, adaptive action
- Stability in Not-Knowing	- Tolerate uncertainty without collapse
- Insight into Automatic Patterns	- Observe habitual thoughts, emotions, and behaviors
- Grounded Clear Seeing	- Recognize impermanence and constructedness

You may notice your reflections naturally touch on one or more of these areas — they are the domains we will explore in depth in the following chapters.

Journaling Template — Applying Step 3

To support practice, use a journal to track Daily Tending, Periodic Alignment, and Deep Cultivation:

1. Daily Tending

- Letting go of: _______________________________
- Reinforcing / supporting: _______________________________
- Necessary / leaving as is: _______________________________

2. Periodic Alignment

- Space or commitments to release: _______________

- Adjustments to pace, boundaries, or priorities: _________
- How I want my overall life flow/garden to feel: _________

3. Deep Cultivation

- Core areas to cultivate (from the 8 areas): ___________
- Tensions or open questions to notice: _______________
- Small actions or experiments to support alignment: ____

This journaling creates feedback loops, helping the gardener see where adjustments are working and where more attention is needed. Over time, these reflections develop stability, clarity, and the capacity to hold not-knowing safely.

Skilful Gardener — Troubleshooting Chapter

As you work with yourself as the skilful gardener, difficulties and blockages may arise. Common examples include:

- Restlessness or overthinking triggered by applying the process
- Drowsiness, heaviness, or lack of energy to apply principles
- Frustration at slow progress and the urge to give up
- Seeing through old programs leading to nihilism or collapse
- Old patterns feeling too strong or too repetitive

These are not new problems—just more sophisticated versions of the original issue: distress and unhappiness driven by old conditioning.

The important move is to recognise, endure, and accept these blockages without giving them extra energy or drama. However, these reactions can be powerful. Alongside recognition and endurance, you can also apply antidotes—common across many traditions and forms of self-development—that support balance and ease. These are outlined below.

TOOLS / ANTIDOTES	
Tool	Function
Self-Observation	Sees what is happening with clarity
Energy	Uplifts and counters dullness
Joy / Lightness	Encourages and keeps engagement
Investigation	Helps understand what is occurring
Tranquillity	Settles heat and emotional charge
Equanimity	Allows without grasping or resisting
Concentration	Steadies attention
Gratitude	Orients to sufficiency
Compassion / Understanding	Softens harshness
Kindness	Humanizes experience
Trust / Confidence	Supports continuation when progress feels slow

TRAPS		
Trap	Description	Useful Antidotes
Desire / Distraction Ill-Will Sloth & Torpor Restlessness & Worry Judgement / Doubt / Shame	Grasping after stimulation Aversion, irritation, blame Dullness, heaviness, disinterest Agitation, unease, anxious busyness Second-guessing or self-attack	Equanimity, Concentration Compassion / Understanding, Kindness Energy, Investigation Tranquillity, Equanimity Self-Observation, Trust / Confidence

How to Use These Antidotes

Antidotes can be developed in formal meditation or in calm contemplation during daily life. What matters is sufficient calm and even-mindedness to observe without reacting.

See these qualities as light, relaxing, supportive, healing, and helpful — and cultivate a sense that they genuinely improve and rebalance you.

These blockages tend to seek drama and over-reaction. Don't feed them energy. Use the same approach you use with the garden: daily tending, periodic alignment, and patient cultivation, bit by bit.

Closing

These obstacles are not failures but signs that conditioning is being touched. Progress often looks uneven from the inside; what matters is tending with continuity rather than force.

The Skillful Gardener Cultivation: Lived Meaning

Rather than starting with answers, this section begins with a clarification. What follows is not an attempt to define "the meaning of life" for you. It is an exploration of how meaning is formed in lived experience. Meaning is not something pre-existing that you uncover once and for all; it develops through how you reflect, choose, and act over time.

Because life keeps changing, any sense of meaning you arrive at is necessarily temporary. New conditions, relationships, and challenges will test what once felt settled. This is not a failure of understanding, but a feature of living wisely. Meaning functions less like a final conclusion and more like an orientation — something you continually refine as you learn how to move through life with greater clarity, responsiveness, and ease.

A skilled gardener first considers meaning: what gives life purpose and direction? As you've seen through the Readiness process, many beliefs we inherited — like chasing success, following rules unquestioningly, or seeking approval — no longer serve us. Through careful reflection, you've decided where you actually stand: some beliefs you keep, others you let go of, and some you remain neutral about.

These decisions reveal your values — the things that feel beneficial and coherent. Beneficial means: they don't harm you or others, they are sustainable over time, and they feel like something you could continue without a sense of obligation or responisbility, or disgeuinity**. For example, helping stray animals can feel naturally motivating: it doesn't harm you or them, and it aligns with what you genuinely care about.

Alignment: Acting Deliberately

Alignment means acting in accordance with your updated values. If wealth isn't meaningful to you, chasing money because others expect it will create tension. If caring for animals feels beneficial, neglecting that to satisfy external expectations will feel out of sync. Alignment is the practice of noticing gaps between what you believe is best and what you're actually doing — and adjusting your actions so they match what you care about.

Actions also have two aspects: the process and the result. There are no fixed rules about which matters more. In some situations, the way you act (the process) is what counts. In others, the tangible benefit (the result) is more important, even if the process was imperfect. Skillfulness is knowing the difference, adapting to circumstances, and responding with clarity rather than compulsion.

Ongoing Refinement

Meaning and alignment are not destinations. Life is unpredictable, and circumstances change. The alignment between your sense of rightness and your actions is an ongoing practice: notice your compulsions, reflect on whether your actions match your values, choose deliberately, and adjust as needed.

At its simplest, the cycle is: notice → reflect → decide → act → adjust. When your actions fit your values and produce benefit, you act not from obligation but from genuine motivation. You feel calm, capable, and resilient, able to face uncertainty without collapsing or scrambling.

Meaning is not something "out there" to be found. It is developed through living deliberately: doing what you've determined is beneficial, acting coherently with your values, and refining as life unfolds. Like a skilled gardener, you cultivate your life through thoughtful, coherent action. Over time, you see that the process itself—this ongoing, adaptive engagement—is where meaning emerges.

Your garden takes the shape you intend.

The Skillful Gardener Cultivation: Discernment of the Beneficial

Before exploring benefit in detail, it helps to reset a common assumption. This discussion does not aim to establish a universal standard of what is beneficial for everyone. Instead, it focuses on how benefit is recognized, tested, and understood within the conditions of your own life. Benefit is not static or guaranteed — it becomes visible through attention, evaluation, and lived consequences.

As circumstances evolve, what once seemed clearly beneficial may lose its usefulness, while something previously overlooked may reveal its value. This ongoing reassessment is not uncertainty for its own sake; it is discernment in action. The aim is not to secure permanent answers, but to cultivate the capacity to respond in ways that are wise, coherent, and sustainable — both for yourself and in relation to others.

Recognizing The Subtlety Of Benefit

A skillful gardener asks: what does it truly mean for something to be beneficial? On the surface, people often treat benefit as fixed and tie it to truth claims or core beliefs. They may say, "Money is beneficial," "Success is beneficial," or "Status is beneficial," acting as if these are absolute.

In reality, what is genuinely beneficial is subtle and personal. Some inherited beliefs contain useful guidance — for example, warnings against greed, envy, pride, lust, or ill will. These are generally non-beneficial behaviors, and noticing them is valuable. Beyond that, we must reflect carefully: not everything labeled "beneficial" by society or tradition actually serves us or others.

Examining Your Own Sense Of Benefit

We can ask ourselves: What do I truly consider beneficial? Then we reflect and examine it carefully. Some modern interpretations — comfort, pleasure, power, or status — may appear compelling but often create inner conflict, stress, or distraction. Conversely, some traditional views — self-denial, strict moral rules, or prioritizing others' needs over your own — may also mislead if they reduce your capacity to act wisely.

A useful marker of benefit is whether your inner world remains steady when the external world is uncertain. Something is beneficial if it helps you respond rather than react, reduces unnecessary conflict, and maintains coherence between your values, actions, and circumstances.

Example: A person may have once believed strict adherence to moral rules defined the "right" way to live and tried to make others follow them. After reflection through the Readiness process, they may realize:

- Following some rules provides structure and personal benefit.
- Enforcing rules on others is not beneficial — it creates stress and harm.

- By stopping attempts to control others, they maximize benefit for themselves and for others.

Benefit In Action

True benefit rarely comes from money, status, or blindly following rules. It comes from actions that:

- Do not harm yourself or others
- Are sustainable and motivating over time
- Create coherence rather than resistance

Practical examples:
- Resting when tired instead of pushing through exhaustion
- Setting boundaries even if others expect more
- Speaking up when necessary, but pausing when reflection shows silence is wiser
- Helping others in ways that genuinely support them without causing harm to yourself

These choices are not fixed prescriptions — they are discernments based on careful reflection. Benefit emerges when your actions align with your considered values, rather than being driven by habit, compulsion, or social pressure.

The Ongoing Practice

For the skillful gardener, determining what is beneficial is an ongoing process:

- Notice your actions, impulses, and drives.

- Reflect on whether they are genuinely beneficial to you and others.
- Decide consciously what to do or not do.
- Act in alignment with your discernment.
- Adjust as new circumstances, experiences, or insights arise.

By practicing this process, you cultivate clarity, calm, and resilience, while acting in ways that serve your life and those around you. Benefit is not a destination — it is discovered through living deliberately, reflecting, and refining.

The Skillful Gardener Cultivation
- Case Study -
Discernment of the Beneficial

Alex is in their early forties and has spent years simplifying life, noticing habitual patterns, and cultivating presence. They are no longer searching for prescriptive rules. Instead, their attention has settled on a quieter, more difficult question: What is genuinely beneficial for me and for those around me?

There are no emergencies in Alex's life, but certain areas have become quietly insistent — not because anyone demands an answer, but because they matter. A long-standing friendship that once felt nourishing now leaves Alex tired and contracted. A career that provides stability and respect no longer aligns with the curiosity and creativity that feel alive in them. The spiritual practices that once guided them now feel more like inherited routines than living expression. Questions about family — children, values, what kind of life they want to cultivate — hover without resolution. None of these questions have simple answers, and none of them can be outsourced to cultural norms or inherited truth claims.

Alex begins by noticing what arises around each possibility. There are the familiar pressures — the internalized shoulds, the subtle anxieties about disappointing others, the impulse to default to tradition or stability. Mixed in with these are quieter signals: curiosity, longing, a sense of alignment that appears for a moment and then disappears again.

Rather than forcing decisions, Alex slows down and watches. They ask themselves what motivations sit underneath certain impulses: Am I leaning toward this choice out of fear? Conformity? Habit? Or because it feels clear, alive, and meaningful? They pay attention to how their nervous system reacts: some options make the body tighten and contract; others introduce a sense of space, steadiness, and possibility. Small experiments are made — a difficult conversation with the friend, a temporary reduction in work hours, a shift toward a more personal mode of practice — not to finalize outcomes, but to gather more information.

As weeks pass, a pattern becomes visible. What is beneficial is not always comfortable, and it rarely aligns perfectly with social expectations. Ending the friendship feels sad, but also relieving. Exploring new forms of creative work feels uncertain, but also energizing. Adapting spiritual practice to something more intimate and less performative feels both unfamiliar and deeply honest. When decisions are made, they are not made by force; they arise when inner and outer conditions line up enough to move.

There is no grand revelation in this process — no final verdict about what is universally good or true. Instead, Alex discovers that beneficiality is contextual and relational. It is felt in the reduction of unnecessary conflict, in the coherence between values and action, in the restoration of curiosity and agency, and in the quiet sense that life is more aligned and less entangled. The work is ongoing, provisional, and alive, and Alex learns to trust the unfolding rather than demand certainty.

The Skillful Gardener Cultivation:
Spiritual Grounding

Spiritual questions often arise naturally in life, whether prompted by curiosity, challenge, or the search for stability and understanding. For the skillful gardener, engaging with these questions is not about discovering fixed truths or definitive answers about God, religion, or the spiritual world. It is about exploring what practices, beliefs, and reflections can support a life that is coherent, beneficial, and compassionate.

Your engagement is always ongoing. At times, certain insights or practices may feel settled; at other times, life will present new circumstances that invite fresh reflection, reconsideration, and adaptation. The purpose is to cultivate a living sense of higher meaning — one that aligns with your values, nourishes your well-being, and supports those around you.

Exploring Spiritual Practices

Spiritual frameworks, whether drawn from religion, philosophy, or contemplative traditions, often exist to meet fundamental human needs:

- Feeling support, love, or acceptance
- Gaining structure, guidance, or stability
- Cultivating compassion and understanding in a complex world
- Seeking fairness, resolution, or relief from suffering
- Accessing tools for transformation and personal growth

For the skillful gardener, the focus is not on unquestioning adoption of these frameworks, but on understanding how they might serve these needs without creating conflict — either internally, with your own values, or externally, with the people and world around you.

Spiritual practices — meditation, prayer, ritual, journaling, acts of service, or contemplative exercises — are tools. They can cultivate calm, clarity, compassion, and connection, but only when engaged with deliberately and reflectively. Some practices will naturally resonate and feel sustaining; others may feel constraining or misaligned. Recognizing this distinction is part of the practice itself.

Reflecting On Benefit And Alignment

A practice is beneficial when it supports your life and the lives of others, rather than becoming a source of compulsion, obligation, or conflict. This can mean noticing:

- How a practice affects your emotional and mental balance
- Whether it aligns with your current understanding of your values and core beliefs
- How it influences your interactions with others and the wider world

Through ongoing reflection, you gradually refine your engagement. Practices are not valuable because they are prescribed by tradition or authority; they are valuable because they fit coherently with your life, sustain your well-being, and help reduce unnecessary conflict.

Example: Someone may have followed strict religious rules because they felt it was necessary to be "good." Through reflection, they might recognize which practices support their well-being and relationships, and which cause stress or tension. They continue what is beneficial, adapt what can be useful, and let go of what creates harm. This process transforms practice from obligation into a source of genuine support and meaning.

- A religious ritual that calms the heart → keep it.
- A religious teaching that creates hatred → let it fade.
- A belief that encourages kindness → keep it.
- A belief that creates superiority → let it fade.

Living With Ongoing Discovery

Engaging with higher meaning is inherently dynamic. Life continually introduces uncertainty, challenge, and new perspectives. The skillful gardener approaches spiritual questions with curiosity, openness, and adaptability, observing how practices and beliefs feel in daily life, integrating what is supportive, and releasing what is not.

This reflective engagement allows spiritual practice to remain responsive, coherent, and nourishing, rather than fixed or dogmatic. It emphasizes process over destination, cultivating wisdom, calm, compassion, and resilience through attentive and intentional participation.

The Skillful Gardener Cultivation:
Relational Grounding

How we relate to others — whether in solitude, intimate relationships, or within a wider community — is never fixed. The skillful gardener notices that these dynamics shift with circumstance, personal needs, and insight. Sometimes, spending a quiet afternoon alone brings clarity and calm, allowing space to reflect on choices or simply rest. At other times, sharing a project with a colleague, listening deeply to a friend, or supporting a family member fosters growth, connection, and a sense of purpose.

Alignment in relationships is an ongoing practice of awareness. The gardener may notice tension when avoiding a necessary conversation, or relief when expressing a need to a partner. They reflect on what is happening: Am I speaking honestly? Am I attending to the needs of others without sacrificing my own? Where do boundaries help preserve clarity and calm? And when is it beneficial to receive support or guidance from others?

Even in solitude, support can be cultivated from within. Journaling about difficult emotions, having a mindful internal dialogue, or pausing to acknowledge one's experience provides guidance and reassurance. Solitude becomes a bridge rather than a barrier, offering space to meet internal needs for acceptance, understanding, and care.

Relationships, whether romantic, familial, or communal, offer similar opportunities. A small conversation about a boundary can strengthen mutual understanding. Volunteering in a local community project can deepen a sense of shared purpose. In each interaction, noticing what feels coherent — when engagement is enriching rather than draining — is central to the skillful gardener's practice.

Neither solitude nor social connection is a fixed state to achieve or avoid. Both are part of a continual practice of alignment. The gardener learns to express themselves authentically, maintain boundaries, accept support when beneficial, and adjust engagement according to the moment. In this ongoing process, calm, clarity, and integrity are preserved — whether alone, with oneself, or with others.

The Skillful Gardener Cultivation: Cultivation of Skillful Living

The skillful gardener does more than act — they choose, direct, and cultivate. They take responsibility for their alignment and well-being while remaining open to learning and change. They do not seek absolute truths or final answers; instead, they pursue clarity that resonates in the present, guiding them toward calm, coherence, and responsive action.

This clarity is not fixed. The gardener lets go of the past — unfinished projects, mistakes, or old habits — like fallen leaves swept aside to make space for new growth. They act conscientiously, without expectation of reward, tending to their inner environment with care. They might pause in the morning to focus on tasks that truly matter, rather than moving on autopilot. They simplify their focus, stay within their bandwidth, and cultivate honesty and integrity, grounding themselves in steadiness and purpose.

Courage is essential. The skillful gardener is willing to make mistakes, speak up even when uncertain, or apologize when they have overreacted. They hold paradox, observe complexity without collapsing, and watch themselves with gentle, attentive awareness. Realignment is always possible; each moment is an opportunity to return to coherence and care.

Inward mastery forms the foundation of skillful living. The gardener loves without expectation, cultivates gratitude and openness, and nurtures intimacy and vulnerability where it is appropriate. They might listen fully to a friend in distress without trying to "fix" them, or take a mindful walk alone to reset after a taxing day. They grow patience, tolerance, and grounded calm, developing deep roots alongside visible flowers. Even on difficult days, when frustration or disappointment arises, they remain steady, embracing uncertainty without judgment, like a tree that bends with the wind but does not break.

Practical attention and reflective awareness are inseparable. Each choice — declining a social invitation that would overextend them, helping a neighbor with care, pausing before replying to a difficult email — contributes to a life of clarity, calm, and thoughtful action. Strength lies not in perfection, but in sustained, conscious engagement with oneself and the world.

Letting Go and Planting New Seeds

Your past is not perfect. It is shaped by the decisions you made with the knowledge and resources you had at the time, often driven by motives that you now recognize were not fully aligned with your well-being. To cultivate a skillful life, you must let the past go. By reflecting on the roots from which your automatic actions sprang, you can see how old conditions influenced your behavior—and now, you are letting those conditions go, planting new seeds in their place.

The clearer you become, removing unhelpful seeds, the more clarity, discernment, understanding, and insight you develop. The result is a beautiful inner garden. This beauty resides within your mind and heart; the external conditions of life remain unpredictable. Tomorrow, you may face illness, loss, or even your mortality—but you will be prepared, not burdened by the past, and aware that the future is uncertain. You will have lived with presence, releasing many mental knots, leaving you in a grounded and resilient place from which to face life.

If you act with compassion, understanding, and for the benefit of others, even in the face of difficulty, you face the future from a place of clarity, calm, and readiness. When life offers joy, you meet it fully; when it offers challenge, you meet it with steadiness and reassurance. To be a skillful gardener is to embody agency, flexibility, and depth. It is to cultivate qualities that stabilize, clarify, and deepen life, while embracing the reality that tending the garden is never complete and that realignment is always part of the practice. Every day offers fresh soil, new shoots, and the ongoing opportunity to nourish the life you wish to live.

The Skillful Gardener Cultivation:
Not-Knowing & Uncertainty

As the skillful gardener deepens their practice, cultivating awareness and alignment with personal agency often leads into uncomfortable and paradoxical terrain. Realigning thoughts, behaviors, and choices with one's clarified values can create tension with people, institutions, or cultural norms that continue to operate under different truth claims. Parents, friends, workplaces, or social groups may respond with disappointment or confusion — not because the gardener has acted harmfully, but because alignment with self-authored values sometimes diverges from established collective narratives.

Navigating this terrain requires the ability to hold paradox and discomfort simultaneously. For instance, a professional may follow strict workplace protocols while privately questioning aspects of those systems. They might follow a procedure that feels outdated, yet gently propose adjustments that reflect a more effective approach. In doing so, they navigate both adherence and critique — acknowledging that both perspectives are valid and necessary.

Similarly, one might honor familial or cultural expectations while acting according to self-authored values that diverge. A person could attend a family dinner out of respect, even if they quietly question certain traditions, while maintaining personal boundaries about what they choose to discuss or participate in. Small choices — joining a social group while limiting emotional energy, or politely declining an invitation — become ways to balance participation with personal alignment, preserving calm and coherence without disengaging entirely.

Within this complexity, values guide action provisionally. The skillful gardener notices whether choices reflect deeper intentions, remaining alert to old habits, external pressures, or ingrained narratives that subtly shape behavior. They might pause before replying to a critical email, choosing words that align with fairness rather than reacting reflexively. Or they may step back from a project that threatens to overextend them, prioritizing clarity, calm, and coherence. Each decision is an opportunity to observe whether alignment is maintained and whether actions cultivate clarity, growth, and benefit for oneself and others.

Ultimately, cultivating the capacity to hold paradox and discomfort is central to self-authorship. It allows honest, responsible engagement with the world without collapsing into rigid adherence, avoiding difficult decisions, or seeking immediate comfort. Discomfort is not a failure; it is a companion on the ongoing journey toward responsive, mindful, and autonomous action. Each moment offers fresh soil, new insight, and the chance to practice steadiness amidst uncertainty.

The Skillful Gardener Cultivation:
Seeing Your Automatic Aspect With Clarity

At Stage 3 of Readiness, the practitioner steps into the role of the skillful gardener, tending the inner landscape of habitual patterns, impulses, and automatic responses — the automatic garden. This garden is not a problem to be fixed, nor a set of rules to follow, but a living terrain to observe, understand, and gently influence. Cultivating it is cultivating awareness, insight, and freedom.

The first task is to see the garden clearly. Patterns repeat without conscious guidance — habits, impulses, and thought tendencies quietly shaping behavior. These may include beliefs like self-blame, entitlement, or automatic tendencies like reductive thinking or over-focus on productivity. Observing them is not self-criticism; it is recognition. Awareness allows the gardener to notice what arises spontaneously and how past decisions were influenced without noticing.

Truth claims — cultural narratives, ideologies, or frameworks — can guide or distort perception. For example, someone might feel compelled to meet social definitions of success even if it drains them. Recognizing these narratives allows the gardener to notice their influence while retaining space for discernment.

Trauma adds another layer. Past wounds can subtly guide reactions or trigger defensive impulses. Awareness illuminates these influences, helping distinguish reactive impulses from intentional actions, and showing where patient, careful cultivation is needed.

Tending the automatic garden also means recognizing the limits of self-determinism. Some degree of automation is necessary — it keeps life stable and preserves mental bandwidth. Change comes slowly, through repeated observation, reflection, and subtle adjustment. Within these limits, the gardener discovers freedom: the capacity to respond thoughtfully, influence patterns, and act in ways that are deliberate, beneficial, and aligned with personal values.

Cultivation is not about perfection. When irritation rises, when habitual worry surfaces, or when a truth claim shapes perception, we notice without being carried away. Reflection helps identify whether impulses stem from fear, habit, conformity, or authentic desire, and how to respond in ways that nurture clarity, presence, and agency. Even small choices — pausing before replying to a text, stepping back from a routine, noticing a reactive thought — become part of this daily practice.

The skillful gardener does not seek total control or eradication of automatic patterns. By observing habits, understanding the interplay of truth claims and trauma, and respecting limits, the practitioner develops the ability to act with clarity, presence, and intentionality. Tending the automatic garden cultivates understanding and freedom — the freedom to respond rather than react, to influence rather than be dominated, and to live with wisdom and care.

In a nutshell, the more you practice READINESS, the more you can see the automatic aspects of your life. Most patterns are fine, but some can be painful. As you progress, you realize that they are all patterns—and all optional. Sometimes you can find a way to shake a pattern; sometimes it clearly isn't you; and other times, it may feel impossible. Remember your mission: you are reclaiming what belongs to you and what you wish to reclaim. It's okay for there to be ups and downs as you make progress. The mission is a worthy one.

The Skillful Gardener Cultivation
- Case Study -
Seeing Your Automatic Aspect With Clarity

Elena, a mid-career professional, has begun practicing Stage 3 Readiness as a Skillful Gardener. She has long noticed recurring patterns in her thinking and behavior: self-doubt, rigid judgments, and habitual anxiety. Some arise from childhood, others from cultural and ideological narratives she has absorbed.

She reflects on a persistent tension: the pull between her religious upbringing and her scientific training. Much of her inner conflict comes from automatically labeling thoughts as "right" or "wrong," "good" or "bad." Recognizing this, she names it in her automatic garden: the impulse to interpret life through rigid truth claims.

Instead of choosing a "correct" perspective, Elena cultivates awareness. She observes the impulses and emotions that arise — anxiety, defensiveness, self-blame — noticing that they stem from habit and external influence, not the situations themselves. She asks: "What is beneficial for me here? What is within my influence, and what must I accept?"

She experiments with a more open approach. She does not need definitive answers or to resolve the tension absolutely. Each thought or impulse becomes a point of reflection, guiding intentional, constructive action.

Over time, Elena notices change. Her impulses remain, but awareness allows her to step back, respond with curiosity instead of defensiveness, and act intentionally rather than compulsively. She participates in discussions without defending a rigid worldview and engages with life with clarity and calm.

Elena's case shows the Skillful Gardener at work: not eradicating patterns or achieving certainty, but observing, reflecting, and making subtle adjustments. The process is ongoing, cultivating wisdom, care, and freedom to act with alignment and presence.

The Skillful Gardener Cultivation: Grounded Clear Seeing

As we progress in Readiness and practice as a Skillful Gardener, we begin to see ourselves and the world with greater clarity. Patterns emerge: habitual thoughts, automatic reactions, and core beliefs become visible. We notice the influence of truth claims — cultural, religious, philosophical, or scientific — which, though intended to guide and stabilize, are always conditional and fallible. They simplify a complex reality, and their usefulness depends on context.

This insight can feel disorienting. If structures we relied on are not absolute, what remains? The practice of clear seeing is not about reaching final answers or discarding guidance. It is about cultivating grounded capacity: the stability to navigate uncertainty, and the discernment to act responsibly even when answers are provisional.

Groundedness and clear seeing develop together. Groundedness lets us face ambiguity without being swept away by doubt or fear. Clear seeing reveals that truths are often partial, sometimes contradictory, yet still meaningful. We observe that a belief may be both helpful and flawed, a system both stabilizing and destabilizing, a choice both beneficial and risky. Holding these tensions is not failure; it is wisdom in action.

Living with open-ended questions requires active engagement. We notice thought and behavior patterns without forcing fixed labels. We reflect on truth claims while discerning which provide guidance. We act with clarity and care, accepting that full certainty is rarely attainable. In this space, absence of final answers is not a void, but a field of possibility where judgment, creativity, and ethical action can flourish.

Ultimately, cultivating groundedness within clear seeing is a practice of balance: acknowledging uncertainty while remaining stable, observing paradox while acting intentionally, recognizing impermanence while focusing on what is truly beneficial. It invites us to live fully and wisely, present and responsive, guided by clarity, care, and the steady cultivation of awareness.

We need to stay grounded in looking for what is beneficial — improving our own lives and the lives of others. When we are not grounded and only see the flaws in all the great truth claims, we risk falling into nihilism. Nihilism is the belief that nothing matters. Taken literally, this might seem true, but experientially it is not. You can make your own experience better, and you can positively impact the lives of others. That is the essence of beneficiality. Getting stuck in nihilism, however, loses sight of this and pits you against yourself and the world. It is an intellectual trap — convincing, but ultimately unworkable.

When you cultivate grounded clear seeing, you come away knowing who you are — not the hopes someone else had for you, but the hopes you have for yourself.

Conclusion:
Becoming the Skillful Gardener of Your Life

At the end of this journey, the picture is clear: life is neither simple nor safe, and the mind is filled with inherited patterns, illusions, and narratives designed to reduce discomfort. Step 1 showed us the garden we inherited, Step 2 gave us the tools and attention to tend it skillfully, and Step 3 has led us into the full practice of being a skillful gardener—one who can navigate the complexities of life with clarity, discernment, and intention.

By now, you know the illusions that once held you captive. You understand that many of the "truth claims" we inherit—from parents, society, or even well-meaning teachers—exist to smooth over the difficulty of life, to make it feel safer or less painful. But life is difficult. No one gets out alive. Each person is unique, faces unique problems, and must find a path that suits their own nature, quirks, and capacities. The truths are provisional; what matters is how you live in the midst of the uncertainty.

Through this work, you've learned to observe your habitual patterns, discern what is beneficial, tolerate not-knowing, cultivate relationships, embody insight, and align your life with meaning and values. You've experienced firsthand that suffering is normal—and that, strangely, we are willing to endure it if it feels meaningful, if it connects to something that matters deeply to us.

Letting go of old programs—the inherited fears, rigid beliefs, and strategies for numbing life—is like discarding the painkillers, quitting the bottle: you experience life unfiltered, awake, and fully. This is not a denial of difficulty; it is the willingness to meet reality as it is, and to act fully within it.

Being a skillful gardener is not about perfection or safety; it is about engaging with life with attention, steadiness, and wisdom. It is about cultivating your unique path, honoring your unique abilities and limitations, and learning to act courageously in the face of impermanence and uncertainty.

At the end of the day, this practice is not about escaping suffering—it is about learning to live in alignment with reality, to engage with life fully, and to embrace your unique role in it, unfiltered and awake. Life is transient, unpredictable, and often challenging. And yet, it is precisely in this openness to the fullness of life—without sedation, without pretense, and with full awareness—that clarity, meaning, and freedom arise.

www.ingramcontent.com/pod-product-compliance
Lightning Source LLC
Chambersburg PA
CBHW080519030726
47592CB00012B/3403